Cat

MISCELLANY

MISCELLANY

FASCINATING FACTS
ABOUT CATS

MAX CRYER

JOHN BLAKE

Published by John Blake Publishing Ltd,
3, Bramber Court, 2 Bramber Road,
London W14 9PB, England

www.blake.co.uk

First published in hardback in 2005

ISBN 1 84454 169 X

British Library Cataloguing-in-Publication Data:

A catalogue record for this book is available from the British Library.

Design by www.envydesign.co.uk

Printed in Great Britain by Creative Print & Design (Wales)

1 3 5 7 9 10 8 6 4 2

Papers used by John Blake Publishing are natural, recyclable products made
from wood grown in sustainable forests. The manufacturing processes
conform to the environmental regulations of the country of origin.

ORIGINAL
ILLUSTRATIONS BY
THE ART OF
LARRY NIELSON

The gifted American artist Larry Nielson is esteemed for his 'nature' depictions – both in his *Spirit of the Wood* creations, and his *Animal* art series.

Nielson's painting on wood of the 1945 US Marines raising the flag on Iwo Jima went to US President George W Bush, and Vice-President Dick Cheney has one of Nielson's original paintings on wood of a buffalo stampede.

Nielson's work appears in several museums and other Nielson art and graphics are owned by Liza Minnelli, Danny Kaye, Johnny Cash, James Brolin, Carol Burnett, Donny Osmond, Georgia Frontiere and Robert Hagel (former President of Warner Brothers).

Nielson was the first Art Director of the Polynesian Cultural Centre in Laie, Hawaii, and was commissioned by the Government of Tonga to paint the official portrait of the late Queen Salote.

During the 1970s and 1980s, his series of animal lithographs were distributed worldwide. These felines are back and available now to a new generation.

The *Cat* series and all other art by Larry Nielson can be seen and are available through: http://windandwings.com/nielson_art.html
Phone *(toll free USA)* 800-548-6448

INTRODUCTION

At various times the cat has been defined as an agile, partly nocturnal, quadrupedal carnivorous mammal, *Felis catus*, with smooth fur and retractile claws, long domesticated as a pet (*Oxford English Dictionary*).

And also:

A furry keyboard cover.

A living alarm clock.

An ego covered with fur.

A small animal frequently mistaken for a meatloaf.

A petite extortionist.

Grace, beauty, mystery and curiosity in a companionable bundle.

Mammal – not large, but with an attitude problem.

Horses carry; dogs retrieve and guard; cows provide milk, meat and hides; sheep are shorn; and lambs and pigs are raised for food. They are all usually described as domesticated animals but, curiously, are seldom perceived as 'part of the family'. The cat, on the other hand, is definitely perceived as part of the family, although it provides nothing.

Nothing?

Not so. The cat keeps human curiosity alert and serves food for the spirit. It suffers no pretensions, is impervious to rank, reduces the self-important to being humble and the aggressive to being calm. Servant to nobody, the cat is choosy about whom it loves, and cannot be persuaded. Many creatures function close to humans: goldfish; guinea-pigs; horses; goats; donkeys; dogs; lambs – but the cat is the only one which can be considered 'free'.

Its form is varied – over 100 recognised breeds and a great many informal outcomes. But, curiously, in spite of the variations, all cats are of a similar size, shape, weight and habit. An alien visitor could instantly recognise any of the hundred breeds as being cousin to the others. This cannot be said about the cat's nearest domestic partner, the dog. Put a Chihuahua next to a Saint Bernard or a spaniel next to an Irish wolf-hound, then tell the alien they are the same thing, and it would definitely be confused.

It would seem impossible to be simultaneously varied and unique – but this quality has been achieved by the cat. And the English language would be far less rich without those contributions that feature it.

Max Cryer, 2005

*'When the world began, the sun created the lion,
and the moon created the cat.'*
ANCIENT GREEK BELIEF

CAT

The word 'cat' appears to have settled down in the English language after a collection of words from both the African and Asian continents contributed to its development. The Nubian *kadis*, the Berber *kadisha*, and *quttah* from North African Arabic may have been factors in the version found in Byzantine Greek: *katta*. In Latin this became *cattus* and *catta*. The Latinate word progressed through ancient German as *kazza* (later *katze*), old Dutch and Frisian as *katte*, old Norse as *kottr* to old French as *cat* (later *chat*) and into old English as *catt*. Then, eventually, *cat*.

'CAT' IN OTHER LANGUAGES:

    Spanish – *gato*
    French – *chat*

Latin – *felida(e)*
Italian – *gatto*
Esperanto – *kato*
Maltese – *gattus*
German – *katze*
Turkish – *kedi*
Russian – *koshka*
Gujarat – *biladi*
Chinese – *mao*
Japanese – *neko*
Swahili – *paka*
Icelandic – *kottur*
Saudi Arabian – *biss*
Greek – *ga'ta*
Ugandan – *paka*
Polish – *kotka*
Romanian – *pisica*
Swedish – *katt*
Hindi – *billi*
Tamil – *pune*
Swahili – *paka*
Korean – *ko-yang-i*
Armenian – *katu*
Dutch – *kattekop*
Hungarian – *macksa*
Hebrew – *KHaTooL' (male)* or *KHa'TooLaH'
(female)*
Maori – *ngeru* or *poti*
Basque – *catua*
Farsi – *gorbe*

Telugu – *pilli*
Zulu – *ikati*
Swahili – *paka*
Estonian – *kiisu*
Finnish – *kissa*
Egyptian – *kut*
Cherokee – *weśa*

'The man who carries a cat by the tail learns something that can be learned no other way.'
MARK TWAIN

The prophet Mohammed, founder of Islam, had a pet cat called Muezza. Legend has it that he loved his cat so much and respected its wish not to be disturbed, that once when Muezza went to sleep on the wide sleeve of his robe, Mohammed gently cut the sleeve off and left it there when he needed to move away, rather than disturb the cat.

'In the middle of a world which has always been a bit mad, the cat walks with confidence.'
ROSEANNE AMBERSON

LIKE A CAT ON A HOT TIN ROOF

Several hundred years ago, before there was any roof made of tin, cats in Britain learned to avoid the *backstone* – or *bake-stone* – a large flat stone at the side of the fireplace on which thin oatcakes and flat scones were baked. Seeking warmth, cats sometimes accidentally stepped on one – but only very briefly. So, by 1683, in parts of Britain's north a person moving quickly might be 'as nimble as a cat on a haite bake-stane'. Within a couple of hundred years, a person in the south would be saying 'Her 'oppeth like a cat 'pon 'ot bricks'.

From meaning just 'speedy', the expression gradually broadened to refer to a person with frayed nerves, ill at ease, uncomfortable and jumpy. When the saying reached America, around 1900, the 'hot bricks' began to give way to a 'hot tin roof'. This version was sealed into immediate recognition in 1955 when writer Tennessee Williams used the expression as the title of his world-famous play.

*'**Cat motto:** No matter what's gone wrong, try to make it look like the dog did it.'*

Angora cats are named after the Turkish city in which they were first found – which later had its name changed to Ankara.

TOMCAT

The term refers to any male cat, but also can refer to a man who enjoys the favours of many women. Until the 18th century male cats were often referred to as 'ram cats'. But in a book written in 1760 in England called *The Life and Adventures of a Cat*, the hero of the book was a male cat with a very active sex life. He was named Tom – and the name (and image) has stuck ever since.

'*If at Christmas you have a dream wherein a black cat appears, then within the following year you will have an illness.*'

GERMAN FOLKLORE

If indeed Noah slammed the ark door on the tail of the last creature to board the ark – a cat from the Isle of Man – then we know why the breed has had no tail ever since. Alas, in a more pragmatic explanation, the Manx cat is a rather unfortunate breed with a genetically deformed backbone that, besides having no tail, affects the shape of the legs. This renders the cat unable to mate with its own kind and produce non-deformed offspring. A tailless Manx cat must always be mated with a tailed one, to prevent the litter being stillborn or misshapen.

There are many fanciful myths about the Manx losing its tail. This little poem brings Noah back into the story – but with a slightly different spin:

Noah, sailing o'er the seas,
Ran fast aground on Ararat.
His dog then made a spring and took
The tail from off a pretty cat.
Puss through the window quick did fly,
And bravely through the waters swam,
Nor ever stopp'd till high and dry
She landed on the Isle of Man.

ANON

*'Cats' hearing apparatus is built to
allow the human voice to easily go in one
ear and out the other.'*
STEPHEN BAKER

Cat owners in England started organising 'showings' of their cats as early as 1861. Then, in 1871, came the first official 'Cat Show' in Crystal Palace, attracting 170 entries and hundreds of visitors and spectators. For the first time, entrants had to be in specific classes and standards – a system that has been practised worldwide ever since. By 1887 Britain had organised a National Cat Club and 1893 saw the publication of the first official cat stud book – serious cat-breeding had begun. Currently the National Cat Show in London (the biggest in the world) attracts over 2,000 pedigree entrants.

America had its first cat show in 1881. By 1895 the event had moved to Madison Square Garden.

*'Mohammed stroked his cat three times
down its spine – thus giving it the power
always to land on its feet.'*
MUSLIM FOLKLORE

LETTING THE CAT OUT OF THE BAG

A secret is revealed – a confidence is broken... the 'cat is out of the bag'. And originally that was quite literal. In earlier centuries when everyone shopped at the market (rather than the supermarket), a live piglet was a desirable purchase for a housewife with a family dinner in view. A vendor would offer a closed, wriggling bag from which squealing could be heard.

But – *caveat emptor* – if the vendor was dishonest, the housewife who innocently took home a squalling, wriggling bag could find a cat inside it (a cat being somewhat easier to come by than a piglet). Another housewife, more discerning, would demand to have the bag opened for viewing before purchase. Either way, when the bag was opened, the vendor's secret was a secret no longer... and the cat was out of the bag. This meaning of 'letting out a secret' came into use in the mid-1700s.

'A pig in a poke' is a closely related saying, *poke* being an old word for 'bag' (its modern descendants are 'pocket' and 'pouch'). Again, the cat hidden in its bag is being passed off as a pig. The aforementioned housewife who didn't look inside the bag until she got home might discover that she had been duped. A pig in a poke is something that is not worth whatever was paid for it. Thomas Tusse mentioned the matter in 1557 in his *Five Hundred Points Of Husbandrie*:

Provide against Michaelmas, bargaine to make,
For farmer to give over, to keepe or to take:
In doing of either, let wit beare a stroke,
for buying or selling, of a pig in a poke.

WAMPUS
American 'Father of the Blues' W C Handy published a band piece called *Wampus Cat Rag* in 1918. 'Wampus' is a mysterious word with various meanings in various contexts. It can describe something large and monstrous, or a person whose behaviour is unpleasant – but sometimes it was used as a compliment like the modern 'cool'. We hope W C Handy was referring to cats in the complimentary sense.

*'Dogs believe they are human.
Cats believe they are God.'*
JEFF VALDEZ

Among hostelries that accept pets, the Cypress Inn in Carmel, California, is recognised as one of the most liberal. Movie star Doris Day – a renowned cat lover – took ownership of the Inn and enhanced its pet services so that cats, dogs and cage-birds are now welcome, pet-sitters are available (cats and dogs may not be left unattended), foods are available for pets (but not for people) and a list is posted of those local restaurants that permit pets to accompany their owners at lunch and dinner.

'When the lion sneezed, the cat was created.'
ARABIAN FOLKLORE

Although unrelated to the Manx, the Bobtail cats of Japan also have no tail. But just to confuse the punter, the lack of tail in the Japanese variety and the similar quality of the Manx relate to two entirely different genetic aberrations, which just happen to produce the same result.

ALL CATS LOVE FISH BUT FEAR TO WET THEIR PAWS

Wanting something of value without wanting to take the trouble or risk to obtain it. The saying existed in medieval times – *Catus amat pisces, sed non vult tingere plantas* – and had drifted into English by 1250: *Cat lufat visch, ac he nele his feth wete.'*

Geoffrey Chaucer knew of the expression. Over two centuries later (c.1606) Shakespeare's Lady Macbeth refers to the same proverb: 'Letting "I dare not" wait upon "I would", like the poor cat i' the adage?'

'Cats are better than any vice. They're not fattening, dangerous or expensive. However... they can be addictive.'

Sir Isaac Newton invented the reflecting telescope and did definitive work on the principles of motion, the discovery of calculus and the principles of gravity. He also invented the cat door!

'Cats do not go for a walk to get somewhere... but to explore.'
SIDNEY DENHAM

A CAT CAN LOOK AT A KING
Based on the observation that, by nature, cats are not obsequious and are certainly not impressed

with anyone's status. Indicating that even the most important of people can be looked at by ordinary folk, the familiar version of the proverb is believed to have originated in Ireland. Other versions exist in other languages: Germans allow that a cat can look at a kaiser (emperor); the French version, however, substitutes the two parties, and has a dog looking at a bishop. In English, the saying appeared in print in 1546 as: 'What, a cat maie looke on a King, ye know' (Heywood).

> Queen Victoria, ever loyal to Scotland, had a favourite cat called White Heather.

*'Cats, flies and women are ever
at their toilets.'*
FRENCH PROVERB

In 1950, a Swiss kitten followed a group of mountain climbers leaving the Hornli Ridge to head up the Matterhorn. To the surprise of the climbers, the kitten later joined them at the Solway hut (12,556 feet up). Surprise turned to astonishment when the kitten gamely battled on, right to the Swiss and then the Italian summit – a climb of 14,000 feet. At the mountain peak, a guide who was aware that cats climb down-wards less easily than they climb upwards put the kitten into his rucksack and took it back to base.

KEYBOARD CATS

Domenico Scarlatti (1685–1757) had a cat called Pulcinella, who was curious about Scarlatti's harpsichord. The sounds made by her walking on its keyboard were eventually developed by the composer into his *Cat's Fugue*.

Over a century later, Chopin was composing his *Waltz No 3 in F major* when his cat also scrambled across the keys of his piano. The composer included a version of the sounds into the waltz – known thereafter as Chopin's *Cat Waltz*.

Twentieth-century American composer Zez Confrey was staying at his grandmother's and was woken in the middle of the night by strange sounds coming from the piano in the parlour. Stumbling downstairs, Confrey found Granny's cat parading up and down the piano keyboard. The incident was turned into a famous 'novelty piano solo' called *Kitten on the Keys* (1921).

Keeping up the good work, in 1962 Brent Fabric came up with yet another hit piano solo, *Alley Cat*.

OTHER CATS IN MUSIC

Stravinsky composed *Lullabies for the Cat.*

Prokofiev used a 'purring' clarinet to represent the cat in *Peter and the Wolf.*

Fauré mimics the frolicking of a kitten in *Kitty Valse.*

Tchaikovsky has a *pas de deux* for two cats in the ballet *Sleeping Beauty.*

Samuel Barber set to song the poem of a 9th-century Irish monk about his cat Pangur.

Rossini's *Duet for Two Cats* is a crowd-pleasing showcase for two sopranos, elegantly recorded by two of the finest sopranos in history – Elisabeth Schwarzkopf and Victoria de los Angeles.

In appearance and behaviour, the hyena seems to suggest relationship with dogs, but is in fact more closely related to the cat family.

'To carry a cat across water in your arms, will bring bad luck.'
FRENCH SUPERSTITION

Cats normally have four kinds of hair: down; awn; guard and vibrissae. Down is thin, short and soft, and sits closest to the cat's body as insulation. Guard hairs are the protective top coat, longer and thicker in structure than down, and arranged so that the underlying coat is kept dry. The awn hair grows between the down and guard hair, and is slightly more bristly. Vibrissae are the whiskers – much longer and tougher hairs than those in the rest of the coat.

'A computer and a cat are somewhat alike – they both purr, and spend a lot of the day motionless. They also have secrets they don't share.'
JOHN UPDIKE

ON A FAVOURITE CAT, DROWNED IN A TUB OF GOLDFISHES

'Twas on a lofty vase's side,
Where China's gayest art had dyed
The azure flowers that blow,
Demurest of the tabby kind,
The pensive Selima, reclin'd,
Gazed on the lake below.
Her conscious tail her joy declar'd:
The fair round face, the snowy beard,
The velvet of her paws,
Her coat that with the tortoise vies,
Her ears of jet, and emerald eyes –
She saw, and purr'd applause.

Still had she gazed, but 'midst the tide
Two angel forms were seen to glide,
The Genii of the stream;
Their scaly armour's Tyrian hue
Through richest purple, to the view
Betray'd a golden gleam.

The hapless Nymph with wonder saw:
A whisker first and then a claw
With many an ardent wish
She stretch'd, in vain, to reach the prize –
What female heart can gold despise?
What cat's averse to fish?

Presumptuous maid! with looks intent
Again she stretch'd, again she bent,
Nor knew the gulf between –
Malignant Fate sat by and smiled –
The slippery verge her feet beguiled;

She tumbled headlong in!
Eight times emerging from the flood
She mew'd to every watery god
Some speedy aid to send: –
No Dolphin came, no Nereid stirr'd,
Nor cruel Tom nor Susan heard –
A favourite has no friend!

From hence, ye Beauties! undeceiv'd
Know one false step is ne'er retrieved,
And be with caution bold:
Not all that tempts your wandering eyes
And heedless hearts is lawful prize,
Nor all that glisters gold!

THOMAS GRAY

A somewhat mysterious organisation called the Museum Of Non-Primate Art fosters knowledge about the 'artistic expression of non-primate species'. This includes (supposedly) moles that tunnel in patterns, horses that release dung into pyramids – and cats that dance and paint. Thought to be located near Chichester, the museum is alas not open to the public, but enthusiastically fosters paintings done by cats and photo-studies of cats dancing on its website, to which contributions arrive from all over the world (www.monpa.com). If a cat shows inhibitions, or any resistance to dancing, MONPA has a special CD available to encourage moggies to do some fancy stepping.

> Movie star Warren Beatty's favourite cat was called Cake.

'Cats do not have to be shown a good time, for they are unfailingly ingenious in that respect.'
JAMES MASON

THE WEEPING WILLOW
Poland claims the legend that changed the shape of riverside willow trees. Centuries ago, when a mother cat's kittens were cruelly thrown into a river, the cat's meowing was so sad that the

willow trees bent their branches down towards the water for the kittens to cling to and be saved. Ever since, willows near water have retained their 'weeping' stance.

> Charles Dickens's white cat, William, surprised him one day by producing kittens. Dickens renamed the cat Williamina.

CATKINS
The name is given to flowers on some varieties of willow and poplar, where many fluffy, non-petalled blooms grow from a long central axis, slightly resembling the tail of a cat.

'Cats are intended to teach us that not everything in nature has a purpose.'
GARRISON KEILLOR

A MODEST CAT'S SOLILOQUY

Far down with the damp dark earth
The grimy miner goes
That I on chill nights may have
A fire to warm my toes;

Brave sailors plough through the wintry main
Through peril and mishap,
That I, on Oriental rugs
May take my morning nap.

Out in the distant meadow
Meekly graze the lowing kine
That milk in endless saucerfulls,
All foaming, may be mine;
The fish that swim in the ocean
And the birds that fill the air –
Did I not like to pick their bones,
Pray, think you they'd be there?
ANON

'Let sleeping cats lie.'
FRENCH PROVERB

CATSILVER

A name given to minerals that separate into thin
leaves – also called 'mica', 'isinglass' and 'glimmer'.

*'Dogs come when they're called, cats take a
message and get back to you later.'*
MARY BLY

Sir Henry Wyatt (born 1460) was a supporter of the Tudors, and thus incurred the unease of Richard III who ordered that Wyatt be imprisoned. He was kept in squalor, tortured and ill-fed. The legend survives that one day a cat appeared at his cell window, dragging a dead pigeon, which it left on the sill. Wyatt persuaded the gaol-keeper to cook the bird, and the cat continued to bring a pigeon for him every day. Sustained in this way, Wyatt survived imprisonment and on the death of Richard III was restored to freedom, grew rich and powerful and was appointed guardian of the prince who became Henry VIII. If the legend about the pigeons is true, one can only hope Sir Henry shared some of his later comfort with the cat that helped him survive to attain it.

'In a cat's eye, all things belong to cats.'

PYEWACKET
In 1644, after keeping a young woman without sleep for four days, British witch-hunter Matthew Hopkins extracted a confession from her that she was indeed a witch. Her 'familiars' were cats, dogs, a rabbit and a ferret, with names including Jamara,

Ilemauzer, Griezzel and Pyewacket. Matthew Hopkins commented that these were names that 'no mortal could invent'. Nevertheless, with or without its history of supposed evil, Pyewacket became current as a popular name for a pet cat.

Three centuries after it was first noticed, the name Pyewacket was reunited with its 'witch' image in 1950 when John Van Druten's hit play *Bell, Book and Candle* opened on Broadway. It told of a beautiful, modern witch (Lilli Palmer) and her equally beautiful 'familiar' cat Pyewacket. The play became a movie starring Kim Novak in 1958.

After that, the name Pyewacket suggested beauty and intrigue rather than evil and, besides naming many pets, it surfaces internationally as a catchy name for some high-class restaurants, an aristocratic racehorse, a rock group, a theatre in Chicago and a luxury charter yacht.

'Nature abhors a vacuum, but
not as much as cats do.'
LEE ENTREKIN

Some cats can jump five times their own height.

CAT'S-TAIL
A marsh-growing plant with long flat leaves, which are used for weaving chair seats and baskets.

22

PUSSY GALORE

The character of Pussy Galore was first introduced to the world by Ian Fleming in his 1959 novel *Goldfinger*. Pussy was leader of a criminal lesbian gang called *The Cement Mixers*. In the 1964 movie version of this James Bond story, Pussy was brilliantly portrayed by Honor Blackman.

> *'It took cats thousands of years
> to domesticate humans.'*
> ANON

Mythology can provide at least one version of how cats first came to Scotland. One of the Pharaohs of Egypt had a beautiful daughter who loved her cats almost as much as she loved her husband, Galthelus, a commander in the Egyptian army. Galthelus was unable to overcome the parting of the Red Sea and left Egypt with a sense of failure, taking his wife the Princess Scota and her cats. They settled in Portugal, but in the following centuries their restless descendants kept travelling North, still taking their cats. Eventually the roaming descendants (and their cats) reached a beautiful land, which became known by the name of their royal ancestor – Scota.

CAT MISCELLANY

'To a dog, you're family. To a cat, you're staff.'

CATSFOOT
A type of ground ivy also known as Haymaids, Creeping Charlie, Hedgemaids and Alehoof. In centuries past it was used to flavour ale, and is still believed to have healing qualities, especially for tinnitus, chronic coughs and indigestion. The plant is poisonous if too much is ingested. (Also known as catspaw.)

> French writer Colette (1873–1954) had two favourite cats called Muscat and Kapok.

C A T ALSO MEANS:
1. Clear Air Turbulence
2. College Ability Test
3. Computerised Axial Tomography (sometimes shortened to CT)
4. Common Assessment Task

'Cats are the ultimate narcissists – you can tell because of the time they spend on personal grooming. Dogs aren't like this – a dog's idea of personal grooming is to roll in a dead fish.'

JAMES GORMAN

> A really healthy cat with a strong impulse to be somewhere else can sprint at 30 miles per hour.

TABBY

This word dates back to medieval Iraq, where a silk fabric with characteristic wavy stripes was manufactured in a district of Baghdad called Attabiyya. An abbreviated form of that name – *Attabi* – became the description of the fabric itself. Eventually the fabric and the name began to be known in Europe, and the Anglicised form 'tabby' drifted into the English language during the 1600s. Initially, it referred only to the luxurious stripy fabric, but, by the end of that century, the name had begun to be used in England to describe cats with a greyish or brownish striped or mottled coat. During the 1700s, a 'tabby' could also mean a gossiping, spiteful woman. Then a complete turnaround in the 1900s saw 'tabby' refer to an attractive young woman. But these uses all faded – the fabric, the pretty young thing and the elderly gossip – and the name tabby to describe certain cats has taken total ownership of the word.

'Was it a car or a cat I saw?'
PALINDROME

OPERATIC CATS

Mozart's comic duet *Nun, liebes Weibchen* (*Now, Dear Wifey*), for two cats, was featured in the opera *The Philosopher's Stone* (c.1790).

Maurice Ravel's children's opera *L'Enfant et les Sortilèges*, with its libretto by Colette, featured a duet by a male and female cat – regarded by scholars as being the first serious treatment in lyric music of cats' love.

> Because it lacks a true collarbone, a cat can take very long steps, curl its front legs, navigate its body through surprisingly small gaps and crouch very close to the ground.

'Nothing's more playful than a young cat, nor more grave than an old one.'

THOMAS FULLER

NIELSON

CLOWDER AND KINDLE

'Clowder' is the correct term for a group of cats gathered together. It is not a word you hear very often, because a gathering of several cats is a fairly rare occurrence. You can see a herd of cows or a flock of sheep any day of the week, but cats don't normally gather in large groups. As a result of this, we don't often need to use the word!

'Clowder' developed from two ancient words, 'clot' and 'clod', which were more or less interchangeable and both meant a shapeless lump. The two words are still around: 'clot' came to be applied to a shapeless lump in liquid (such as in milk or blood); 'clod' referred to a shapeless lump of something solid (such as soil). But from 'clod' came the word 'clodder', which was used to describe a shapeless, disorganised mass or group accompanied by pandemonium and even noise.

By the late 19th century four derivatives of the two original words had settled into contemporary English:

'clot' – a shapeless lump but usually associated with liquid;

'clod' – another shapeless lump, usually solid;

'clutter' – a disorganised collection of objects, which in general remained still;

'clowder' – an untidy assembly of objects which did not remain still but moved around and possibly even made noise.

So, although 'clowder' is connected to 'clutter',

over the centuries 'clutter' has come to mean a messy collection of stationary things (think of a table after a four-course meal, or a teenager's bedroom) while 'clowder' describes a group of objects or living creatures moving around independently of each other.

Therefore, 'clowder' is the perfect word to describe an assembly of cats.

A KINDLE OF KITTENS
A very old use of the verb 'to kindle' meant 'to give birth', and was usually applied to small creatures. This gave rise to the expression 'a kindle of kittens'.

> Tennis champion Jimmy Connors had a cat called Kismet.

When the British Consul to Siam, Owen Gould, was due to leave Bangkok in 1884, King Chulalongkorn (tutored as a boy prince by Anna Leonowens) presented Gould with two Siamese cats as a farewell present. Until then, Siamese cats were only ever owned by the royal family or the upper level of Thai aristocracy, and had never been seen in Britain. Gould's sister, Mrs Veley, exhibited the pair at Crystal Palace in 1886 – and cat fanciers fell in love with them immediately.

> '*If man could be crossed with a cat, it would improve the man but deteriorate the cat.*'
> MARK TWAIN

The human sense of smell is only one-twelfth as sensitive as that of a cat, which has 67 million olfactory cells. The cat can also 'create' scents from tiny glands on its face, tail and paws. A gentle brush against something (including a human) can leave a slight scent which the cat can later 'read' for itself – or convey as information for other cats.

FROM *THE HISTORIE OF FOURE-FOOTED BEASTS*, 1607

A Cat is a familiar and well knowne beast... Ovid saith, that when the Gyantes warred with the Goddes, the Goddes put upon them the shapes of Beasts, and the sister of Apollo lay for a spy in the likenes of a cat, for a cat is a watchfull and warye beast... And for this cause did the Egyptians place them for hallowed Beasts, and kept them in their Temples... and not onely the Egyptians were fooles in this kind, but the Arabians also, who worshipped a cat for a God; and when the cat dyed, they mourned as much for her, as for the father of the family...

EDWARD TOPSELL

29

'One is never sure, watching two cats washing each other, whether it's affection, the taste, or a trial run for the jugular.'
HELEN THOMSON

Cats cannot actually see in total darkness, but the structure of a cat's eyes allows it to see quite clearly in only one-sixth of the light that humans need to see clearly. In near-darkness, things barely visible to a human can be distinguished quite easily by a cat.

ALLEY CAT
A stray or homeless cat, with a tough disposition, a firm level of self-preservation and a somewhat elastic set of morals. The term is also often applied to a person of similar qualities – and is not a compliment. The 'alley' portion may evoke the image of prostitutes, who used to lurk in alleys – sometimes carrying their own mattresses. The 'cat' probably alludes to the take-on-all-comers habits of female cats when they're in mating mood.

'When the mouse laughs at the cat –
there is a hole nearby.'
NIGERIAN SAYING

In old Siam, when a member of the royal family died, a tomb was prepared with a series of holes that led from the casket eventually to the outside air. A live Siamese cat was buried with the royal body. When the cat finally navigated its way through the holes, and emerged into the outside air (as it always did), the populace then knew that the royal soul had been released.

CATWOMAN

The sleek figure of Catwoman was first seen in the 1940 magazine cartoons of Bob Kane, who had originated Batman in the *Detective Comics* a year earlier. She started out as a burglar and adversary of Batman, but Catwoman's character gradually developed a more sexy image and a possible romantic interest for Batman.

Besides magazine comic strips, Catwoman has been seen in animated movies and on both small and big screen – played on television by Julie Newmar and then Eartha Kitt (1967), and in movies by Lee Meriweather (1966), Michelle Pfeiffer (1992) and Halle Berry (2004).

Leonardo da Vinci often sketched cats, both in motion and at rest. His painting *Madonna and Child with a Cat* shows Jesus holding a kitten firmly as if to prevent it running from him.

NOT ENOUGH ROOM TO SWING A CAT

The English language is such a polyglot, and has so much imagery coming into everyday use from widely differing sources, that quite often rival explanations develop of exactly where and how an expression developed.

Such is this one: like distant family claiming a celebrity, five different sources lay claim to be the ancestor of the saying 'not enough room to swing a cat'.

The most usually accepted is that the 'cat' referred to isn't a cat at all, but is the whip used for punishment in the old sailing ship days, the dreaded cat-o'-nine-tails. When wielded on a misbehaved sailor's back, the whip's nine knotted thongs provided a most painful experience. But to put this into effect, the whip's swinger needed room – more than the average ship cabin provided. So whippings were customarily carried out on deck, not only to demonstrate to the rest of the crew the consequence of evil ways, but also because the space on deck allowed room to 'swing a cat' – which the cabin did not.

There is, however, some doubt about this

explanation, because of the view that 'no room to swing a cat' existed as an expression a hundred years before the cat-o'-nine-tails came into use. So explanation number two moves into place – and it is another unpleasant one.

The belief that cats had mysterious and evil powers associated with witchcraft, and should therefore be tortured and killed, was rampant at roughly the same time as when the battles within Europe required expert archers. For target practice someone would in fact swing a cat, which the archer then tried to hit with an arrow. This activity obviously needed a lot of space. If the cat wasn't literally swung by its tail (a little dangerous for the swinger when facing a less-than-adept archer), it could be put into a sack or leather wine container, hung from a branch and then set swinging.

Shakespeare refers to it in *Much Ado about Nothing* (1598), when Benedict says, 'Hang me in a bottle like a cat and shoot at me.'

Charles Dickens seems to favour a similar concept in *David Copperfield* (1850). When the character of Mr Dick uses the term, his meaning appears to be quite literal: 'You know, Trotwood, I don't want to swing a cat. I never do swing a cat.'

Back to sea for adherents of the third explanation, who affirm that in this case 'cat' is a corruption of 'cot', a shipboard term describing a form of hammock which required space in which to be properly hung.

Explanation number four remains with the sea, where the term 'cat' can describe a compact merchant vessel. If a mooring did not have enough space for such a vessel to manoeuvre, then there was 'not enough room to swing a cat'.

Finally, there's the fifth explanation. In certain Scottish dialects, a 'cat' was a 'rogue' who, when he ran out of luck, would come to his end with a noose. The cat's hanging would have needed a certain amount of room.

At least, amid the various tangles of its ancestry, the meaning of the expression has remained comfortingly stable and clear: 'not enough room to swing a cat' is undoubtedly referring to a small area.

So fastidiously clean is the cat that, it has been estimated that during its life the average cat spends 30 per cent of the time grooming itself. In doing so, it loses almost as much fluid as it loses in urine.

'No matter how much cats fight, there always seem to be plenty of kittens.'
ABRAHAM LINCOLN

Aspirin is poison to cats.

In the Oriental lunar calendar still followed by the Chinese, a cycle of 12 years allocates each

year into the guardianship of a different animal. The cat is notably absent. Many legends abound as to why the cat was omitted from the list (originally made by the Buddha). Some kind of altercation between the cat and the rat features in most versions of the story, or that the rat had once fetched medicine for the Buddha when he was ill, but the cat – not knowing this – later caught the rat and ate it. But the legend that most cat-lovers favour says that when the Buddha gathered all the animals together in order to make his choice of twelve, the cat was asleep and missed the meeting.

*'A cat sneezing is a good omen
for everyone who hears it.'*
ITALIAN FOLKLORE

CAT-LAP
A scornful name for a soft or non-alcoholic drink, something mild which a cat might lap, such as weak tea. A youth might be described as not yet old enough to drink anything except cat-lap. Sir Walter Scott mentions it in *Redgauntlet* (1824): 'A more accomplished old woman never drank cat-lap.'

Cats can sweat – but only through their paws.

36

TOBEMORY

Unlike the rest of the cats in the world, who communicate vocally and with varied body language, Tobermory has the unusual ability to speak English. This he does at an upper-class weekend party, to the amazement of the guests, in Saki's *Chronicles of Clovis* (1911).

'It is easier to hold quicksilver between finger and thumb, than to keep a cat who means to escape.'
ANDREW LANG

ENOUGH TO MAKE A CAT LAUGH (OR SPEAK)

It can generally be agreed that cats don't laugh. It would have to be something extremely humorous to persuade them towards even a faint snigger. It follows, then, that 'enough to make a cat laugh' indicates an event or possibility so ludicrous that it might even stir a cat to giggle. And because cats also do not normally talk (at least not in English), something that could 'make a cat speak' (rather than laugh) generally refers to strong drink, which tends to loosen tongues. Shakespeare mentions it in *The Tempest*: 'Who is it but loves good liquor? 'Twill make a cat speak.'

CAT MISCELLANY

Cat proverb: Never sleep alone when you can sleep on someone's face.

THE KITTEN AND THE FALLING LEAVES

That way look, my infant, lo!
What a pretty baby-show!

See the kitten on the wall,
sporting with the leaves that fall.
Withered leaves – one – two and three
from the lofty elder tree.
Though the calm and frosty air

of this morning bright and fair.
Eddying round and round they sink,
softly, slowly; one might think.
From the motions that are made,
every little leaf conveyed
Sylph or Faery hither tending,
to this lower world descending.
Each invisible and mute,
in his wavering parachute.

But the Kitten, how she starts,
crouches, stretches, paws, and darts!
First at one, and then its fellow,
just as light and just as yellow.
There are many now – now one,

now they stop and there are none:
What intenseness of desire,
in her upward eye of fire!

With a tiger-leap half-way,
now she meets the coming prey.
lets it go as fast, and then;
Has it in her power again.
Now she works with three or four,
like an Indian conjuror.

(ABRIDGED) WILLIAM WORDSWORTH

'As busy as a cat in a tripe shop.'
19TH-CENTURY ENGLISH SAYING

CATHOUSE

This slang term for a brothel is derived from the ancient (15th-century) use of the word 'cat' as a derisive term for prostitute, drawn from the observation that, when a female cat is in heat, male cats feel compelled to gather around her.

'When I play with my cat, who knows if I am not a pastime to her, more than she is to me?'
MONTAIGNE

In Korea, a very tigerlike cat called Hodori has been familiar in folklore and legends for decades. In 1988 he became the symbol for the Seoul Olympic Games.

CATSUIT

The catsuit, a form-fitting garment covering the whole body all in one piece, is thought to have derived its name from the costume customarily worn by a pantomime 'cat' – usually a slim dancer in a sleek, close-fitting disguise. The garment leapt to prominence in 1964 when Diana Rigg made a memorable impact on television viewers in *The Avengers*. Her character, Mrs Emma Peel, was not playing a cat, but in Britain the image of the young Ms Rigg became allied with her shapely, high-fashion catsuits. Not long after Diana Rigg came onto the television screen, American TV viewers were introduced to a similarly clad Catwoman, played by Julie Newmar in *Batman*, and the catsuit was here to stay.

FROM AMBROSE BIERCE, *THE DEVIL'S DICTIONARY*

CAT, *n.* A soft, indestructible automaton provided by nature to be kicked when things go wrong in the domestic circle.

Unlike humans, cats appear to wash themselves *after* they've had a meal. According to an old legend, once when a sparrow was caught in a cat's claws, it chided the cat for planning to eat it without first washing its own paws and face. Embarrassed, the cat prepared to wash, temporarily putting the sparrow down. But the sparrow, taking advantage of the 'temporary' freedom, immediately took the opportunity to fly away. From this time on, cats have always eaten first and washed later.

> It is believed that Cleopatra had a favourite cat called Charmain.

RUB SOMEONE THE WRONG WAY
Irritate or upset a person. A reference to the annoyance caused to a cat which has its fur stroked backwards.

'The moving cat sheds and, having shed, moves on...'

H G WELLS
Wells is generally regarded as the world's first great writer of science fiction, and not known to have

any particular relationship with cats. But, according to his famous novel *The Invisible Man* (1897), the project to make a man invisible could not have occurred without one. The character of his scientist Griffin admitted that he'd first tried out the drug involved on a cat. It had almost been a success – but the cat's eyes had moved around the room in ghost-like fashion without the cat's body being visible around them.

CAT BALLOU
In this 1965 hit movie Jane Fonda played Catherine Ballou, known as 'Cat' – a young schoolteacher setting out to avenge the murder of her father.

'Rats don't dance in the cat's doorway.'
(Meaning 'don't push your luck!')
AFRICAN PROVERB

SOURPUSS
Someone who is cranky. Some scholars assign the word's ancestry to an ancient word 'buss' which at the time referred to the face. Over time, the word

may have undergone a change in pronunciation (see **Puss**).

KIT-KAT CLUBS

Two such venues have had notable literary association. The 17th- and 18th-century London bookseller Jacob Tonson began a series of meetings in the premises of Christopher ('Kit') Catt – a maker of mutton pies. Known as the Kit-Kat Club, its 39 members included political and literary celebrities of the time. Mr Catt's premises had a low ceiling and its walls could only accommodate paintings that were wider than they were high. For a time, paintings of this oblong shape were referred to as 'kit-kats', whose determinedly oblong shape is believed (several centuries later) to be the origin of the name of a similarly shaped chocolate bar.

Christopher Isherwood's collection of stories *Goodbye To Berlin* was published in 1939, introducing readers to another 'Kit-Kat Club' – a murky dive in 1920s Berlin, employing an English singer of alternative lifestyle called Sally Bowles. The original book was turned into a play (*I am a Camera*, 1951), then a stage musical (*Cabaret*, 1968) and eventually a film of the musical (1972). The film made extraordinary changes to large amounts of the original story, including changing the nationality of the leading character – but the Kit-Kat Club retained its seediness.

'Cats are kindly masters – just as long as you remember your place.'
PAUL GRAY

CAT PEOPLE
Cat People is a 1942 horror movie (directed by the esteemed Jacques Tourneur) about a Serbian-born fashion artist in New York. She carries an ancient curse that causes her – when emotionally aroused – to turn into an avenging panther! The film was remade by Paul Schrader in 1982. It starred Malcolm McDowell and Nastassja Kinski.

GET ONE'S BACK UP
Show anger or annoyance. The allusion is to a cat, which arches its back when threatened by a dog or other animal in order to make itself look bigger.

'My husband said it was him or the cat.
I miss him sometimes.'
ANON

> The Oxford Union Society discourages dogs
> in its London premises, and imposes a fine if
> one is brought in. But reputedly there is a
> 'Rule 46' within the Union, which declares
> that 'any animal leading a blind person shall
> be deemed to be a cat'.

THAT DARN CAT!

Based on the book *Undercover Cat* by Gordon and
Mildred Gordon, the 1965 movie *That Darn Cat!*
tells the story of a wise cat working with top-
ranking security agents to catch law-breakers.
Actors Hayley Mills and Roddy McDowall helped.

'A cat with kittens nearly always decides, sooner
or later, to move them.'
SIDNEY DENHAM

CATFISH

A fish family classified as *silurids* with many
varieties, featuring sensory barbels around the
mouth (resembling the whiskers of a cat) and a
skin with no scales.

OCTOPUSSY

Ian Fleming's story *Octopussy*, published in 1966, has nothing to do with cats. James Bond is depicted up against the forces of evil, as usual, this time including a beautiful smuggler known as Octopussy. Maud Adams played the role in the 1983 movie.

THERE ARE MORE WAYS TO KILL A CAT

Confusion has reigned about this expression since the first basic manifestation appeared in John Ray's *A Collection of English Proverbs* in 1670. Variations have cropped up in the examples offered of how a cat *might* be killed – for example, choking it with cream, choking it with butter or simply choking it to death. The version using the word 'kill' was quite well established by the mid-1800s, and can be found in Charles Kingsley's *Westward Ho!* (1855). The basic intention of the expression seemed to be to point out that there can be several ways of accomplishing a desired objective, with perhaps a subtle indication that a stronger application might be needed (rather than wasting a lot of cream).

However, the proverb has now been largely superseded by 'there is more than one way to skin a cat'. This variation on the earlier use of 'kill' began to appear in the mid-1800s, and occurs in Seba Smith's *Yankee Life* (1854), and then in Mark Twain's *A Connecticut Yankee in King Arthur's Court* (1889).

But in America, the term 'skinning a cat' has at least two other connotations. It describes a gymnastic exercise – hanging on a branch or cross-bar, then drawing the feet and legs up through the arms and hauling the body weight upwards to finish sitting on the horizontal (an effect to the viewer which is rather like 'skinning' a creature!).

But the main American claimant to the expression's ancestry is not a cat, but a catfish. Unlike most other fish, a catfish, which has whiskers, needs to be skinned (not just scaled) before it can be cooked and eaten. Among communities that catch and eat their own fish, various groups have different ways of skinning their catch, which they customarily refer to as just a 'cat' rather than a 'catfish'. Given that the basis of the expression dates back at least to 1678, however, the application to fishing might be add-on rather than origin.

At least amid the language confusion there is some comfort in the fact that none of it concerns actually skinning a real cat.

COPYCAT

A person who copies others. Undoubtedly a reference to the way kittens learn from their mothers by being shown an action, then copying it.

Cats sleep on average between 14 and 18 hours a day.

'Whether they be real cats or the musician cats in my band – they all got style!'
RAY CHARLES

PANCHATANTRA

This large collection of animal fables was composed many years BC in the Sanskrit language. It is believed that, in a later century, an Eastern prince ordered it to be translated in Pahlavi so that his three sons could be educated in both manners and morals. The fables were eventually turned into Arabic, then Greek and Latin, and in 1570 Sir Thomas North translated them into English.

One of the fables, 'The Lean Cat and the Fat Cat', refers to a cat's supposed nine lives. It tells of a humble old lady who lived in a cottage, whose pet cat was fed scraps and home-made broth. One day the cat met a plump and sleek puss who persuaded him that a fine meal could be had by stealing morsels from the king's table.

Defying the advice of the poor old woman, the lean cat sneaked into the palace. It did not know that the king had already become so fed up with cats stealing his meals that on that very day he had decreed that all cats entering the dining hall should be killed. The fat cat had already heard this and stayed away, but the lean cat padded in and was immediately attacked. He lay still and feigned death, swearing that, if he escaped, he would remain faithful to his honest owner for the rest of his nine lives. Reunited with the old woman, they agreed upon the moral: 'Stay where you are safe, and the broth is honest. Steal and you court your doom.'

'The cat is in the clock!'
(Meaning: if the husband and
wife argue, the cat hides!)
BELGIAN PROVERB

A SCORCHED CAT FEARS EVEN A COLD STOVE

Learning a lesson, but not always applying the wisdom correctly and becoming over cautious as a result. There are various versions, the earliest sighting in English being in 1611 – 'The scalded cat fears even cold water' – and there is a similar concept in an Arabic saying: 'A cat bitten once by a snake dreads even rope.'

There are about 30 muscles in a cat's ear (a human has six). Each ear can be rotated separately through 180 degrees – thus detecting and analysing noises from two directions simultaneously.

'Do not meddle in the affairs of cats, for they are subtle and will pee on your computer.'
BRUCE GRAHAM

A CAT I KEEP

A cat I keep
That plays about my house,
Grown fat with eating
Many a miching* mouse.
ROBERT HERRICK

MONEY CATS
There is no strict rule about the saying 'money cat', but generally it describes 'piebald' cats,

*(*miching* – an old word for lurking, hiding)

whose fur has any combination of three colours. In America, the expression is interchangeable with 'calico cat', again meaning a cat with three colours (in some countries, calico is a plain fabric, but early-American calico was often multi-coloured).

The only known story behind the term 'money cat' dates back to an ancient Dutch legend about a poor milkman whose clients collected their milk and left their payment of coins pushed under his door. Thieves learned to flick the coins out again, using a rose-bush stem. But the milkman's multi-coloured cat learned a trick, too. When the coins appeared under the door, she pawed them out of reach and, if a rose stem appeared probing around, she seized it and ripped it away from the thieving hands. The milkman received all the money due to him, thanks to his 'money cat' – and then everyone in the village wanted one, too!

THE THREE LIVES OF THOMASINA

Based on a book by Paul Gallico, this whimsical 1964 film is about a young girl's pet cat, which dies after attention from a veterinarian. However, it comes under the influence of a beautiful contemporary witch who has skills at reviving the dead. Patrick McGoohan and Susan Hampshire starred.

*'The trouble with cats is that
they've got no tact.'*
P G WODEHOUSE

> When scents waft in through a cat's open mouth, they are received on the roof of the mouth by the highly sensitive Jacobson's organ, which conveys the scents' messages to the brain. Using this, one cat can detect another cat as far away as 100 metres.

THE ORIENTAL MONEY CAT

Japanese folklore tells of when, during the 17th century, the Gotoku-ji temple outside Tokyo was beset by poverty. But the Buddhist abbot loved cats and, no matter how difficult it was to keep them fed, he looked after his pets. One day he told the cats that a serious crisis now loomed – good luck was needed, and some income was essential, or the temple would have to be disbanded.

Soon, some samurai warriors were passing and saw a cat with its paw upraised, which the warriors interpreted as a greeting. They took it as an invitation to stop and rest, because a storm had arisen. The warriors took shelter in the temple and, to reward the abbot for his hospitality, the samurai warriors became benefactors of the temple, restoring it to wealth and honour.

From then on, the cat with its paw upraised became a symbol for good luck and good fortune.

The Gotoku-ji temple now contains a statuette of its original benefactor cat – and many other cat tributes as well. Visitors go there to pray that the cat will bring them the same luck and prosperity it brought to the monks of the past. Models of the original cat – with paw upraised – are called 'Maneki Neko' and can often be seen in Japanese homes, shops, businesses and restaurants. Sometimes its raised paw is waving; a discreet internal battery helps to draw the good fortune towards itself and into the premises. Besides Japan, the 'money cat' or 'good fortune cat' has been adopted in other places in the East and in Oriental places of business worldwide.

The Maneki Neko cats can be made of porcelain, wood, metal, ivory or pottery, and are usually red-and-gold or black-and-white. Besides being harbingers of fortune, they often also serve a second duty – as money boxes.

'Buds will be roses and kittens,
cats – more's the pity.'
LOUISA MAY ALCOTT

'Who could believe such pleasure
from a wee ball o' fur?'
IRISH SAYING

A cat's skin secretes a kind of 'sweat' containing the chemical *cholecalciferol*. When a cat is lying in the sun, the sunlight converts that chemical into Vitamin D. When a cat lies in the sun it often licks its fur, therefore effortlessly putting the Vitamin D into its system and helping keep up its energy levels.

PUSS IN BOOTS

This familiar figure has appeared in European legends for centuries – he can be found in Italian folk tales of 1554. Over a century on, the famous collection of fables and legends, collected and retold by French writer Charles Perrault in 1697, was published in English in 1729 as *Tales from Mother Goose*. Included was the *Puss in Boots* story familiar to English-speaking children ever since, about the clever cat who helps his master secure a fortune – and a beautiful bride. A statue of Puss in Boots is part of the monument to Charles Perrault in the Jardin des Tuileries, Paris.

'Giving a cat a bath is a martial art.'

MAKE THE FUR FLY

An altercation – not necessarily physical, but certainly spirited. Some think the saying developed from the nursery poem *The Duel* by Eugene Field – which doesn't actually mention fur flying but certainly puts across a similar image, as in this excerpt:

The air was littered, an hour or so,
With bits of gingham and calico,
While the old Dutch clock in the chimney-place
Up with its hands before its face!
But the gingham dog and the calico cat
Wallowed this way and tumbled that,

Employing every tooth and claw
In the awfullest way you ever saw –
And oh! how the gingham and calico flew! (1890)

'Cats regard people as warm-blooded furniture.'
JAQUELYN MITCHARD

NOT TO HAVE A CAT IN HELL'S CHANCE

This is a contraction of the original, slightly longer version 'No more chance than a cat in hell without claws'. Either way, it has developed a strong image of a situation being hopeless. Dropping reference to the 'weapons' in the shortened version doesn't seem to make much difference – surely the poor cat would be doomed anyway? Two modern additions to the expression seem to give it an even more ominous tone: 'No more chance than a celluloid cat in hell' or '... wax cat in hell'.

*'Purr and the world purrs with you.
Hiss and you hiss alone.'*

MINERVA MCGONAGALL

Dame Maggie Smith plays Minerva McGonagall in the *Harry Potter* movies. In the first, *Harry Potter and the Philosopher's Stone* (2001), Dame Maggie's first appearance is as a cat that, before one's very eyes, changes into Ms McGonagall, senior Professor at Hogwarts School for wizards. She is able to turn herself into a cat at will, and does so a couple more times in the same film.

'Fair-haired little girls, books, and cats make the best furniture for a room.'
FRENCH PROVERB

THIS IS THE HOUSE THAT JACK BUILT

The poem *This is the House that Jack Built* may date as far back as the 13th century, and its 'accumulative' structure may be based on an ancient Hebrew chant about a kid-goat that is bought for two farthings. By 1750, when it first appeared in print, *The House that Jack Built* may have been referring to a mythical character called John Bull. But, whatever its mysteries, the poem certainly features the lines:

This is the cat
That killed the rat
That ate the malt
That lay in the house that Jack built.

CATTY REMARKS
Unkind comments, often (but not always) made by a woman and often (but not always) about another woman. A vague association between women and cats has been around for centuries, and gained wider currency in the 1500s when Heywood collected the saying 'a woman hath nine lives like a cat'. Soon, a woman who gossiped about other women was said to be making catty remarks.

'If a cat washes behind its ears, there will be rain.'
BRITISH FOLKLORE

RHUBARB
The 1951 movie *Rhubarb* tells of an eccentric millionaire who leaves his fortune – and ownership of a baseball club – to a cat. Alas, the club's manager and publicist has a fiancée who is allergic to cats...

CAT MISCELLANY

*'Anger improves nothing except the angle
of a cat's back.'*

There are two notable Cat Museums. In Malaysia, a 1987 exhibition of 'cat artefacts' in the Kuala Lumpur Museum was taken to Kuching (the 'Cat City') under the care of the Sarawak Museum, and is now established as a totally independent Cat Museum. Regarded as a 'Cat Information Centre', the museum is situated on a hill with magnificent views, and encourages meetings between cat enthusiasts and researchers.

In Russia, the Moscow Cat Museum has a vast collection connected with cats in life and in art, including paintings, graphics, batiks, tapestries, collages, costumes, calendars, postcards, albums, ceramics, sculptures, glassware, dolls and photography. It has more than 1,500 items and is being constantly expanded. Besides these, books, souvenirs, photographs, films, cartoons and toys abound, all connected with cats. There are songs about cats, cat film festivals, theatre and dance groups, cat 'fashion shows' and an annual beauty contest called 'Woman and Cat', in which the jury evaluates the beauty and grace of the pair. Also, at least once a year, an exhibition is mounted of children's paintings of cats. The museum tours parts of its collection throughout Russia and occasionally to other countries.

*'I gave an order to the cat, and the
cat gave it to its tail.'*
CHINESE SAYING

CHANG TUAN
The scholar Chang Tuan of ancient China gave his
cats very colourful names: Purple Blossom; Drive-
Away-Vexation; Guardian of the East; Brocade
Sash; Cloud Pattern and White Phoenix.

'Macrobiotic cats eat only brown mice.'

BOSWELL ON DR JOHNSON
I never shall forget the indulgence with which he
treated Hodge, his cat: for whom he himself used
to go out and buy oysters, lest the servants having
that trouble should take a dislike to the poor
creature ... I recollect [Hodge] one day scrambling
up Dr Johnson's breast, apparently with much
satisfaction, while my friend smiling and half-
whistling, rubbed down his back, and pulled him
by the tail; and when I observed he was a fine cat,
saying 'why yes, Sir, but I have had cats whom I
liked better than this;' and then as if perceiving
Hodge to be out of countenance, adding, 'but he
is a very fine cat, a very fine cat indeed'.
JAMES BOSWELL, THE LIFE OF SAMUEL JOHNSON (1791)

HODGE'S STATUE

In Gough Square, London, Dr Samuel Johnson's cat Hodge, who died c.1784, has its own life-size bronze memorial statue. It was unveiled in September 1997 by the Lord Mayor of London, Sir Roger Cook, and shows Hodge sitting on a dictionary. Percival Stockdale wrote *An Elegy on the Death of Dr Johnson's Favourite Cat*, from which we learn that Hodge was a black cat:

> Who, by his master when caressed
> Warmly his gratitude expressed;
> And never failed his thanks to purr
> Whene'er he stroked his sable fur.

'How we behave towards cats here below, determines our status in Heaven.'
ROBERT A HEINLEIN

ROMEO AND JULIET

A bizarre movie version of Shakespeare's *Romeo and Juliet* was made in 1990, featuring a cast made up entirely of cats. The project took over a year to film, mainly on the streets, and voices were supplied by an all-star cast including Vanessa Redgrave, Ben Kingsley, John Hurt and Dame Maggie Smith.

*'I could endure anything before but a cat,
and now he's a cat to me.'*
BERTRAM, FROM SHAKESPEARE'S *ALL'S WELL
THAT ENDS WELL*

*'There are many intelligent species in the universe.
They are all owned by cats.'*

Cats easily see things at a distance, but sometimes not so well close-up (especially something right underneath their nose). The whiskers act as navigators and sensors of distance, detectors of air currents (revealing tiny movements nearby, such as those of a mouse), and let the cat know whether an opening is wide enough for its body to get through. The whiskers themselves are simply thickened hair – but are deeply rooted in highly sensitive nerve tissue that can convey a mass of information. There are usually 24 whiskers, and they can be moved forwards, backwards and downwards.

Many white cats with blue eyes are deaf.

*'There are two means of refuge from the
miseries of life – music and cats.'*
ALBERT SCHWEIZER

LOOK WHAT THE CAT DRAGGED IN

A slightly derogatory comment made on a person's arrival. An obvious reference to the cat's tendency to bring home its prey, tattered and torn, after 'playing' with it for a while.

> *'Some say cats are devils, but they behave badly only when they are alone. When they are among us, cats are angels.'*
>
> GEORGE SAND

FROM *THE JOURNAL OF A VOYAGE TO LISBON, 1755*

A most tragical incident fell out this day at sea. While the ship was under sail, but making as will appear no great way, a kitten, one of four of the feline inhabitants of the cabin, fell from the window into the water: an alarm was immediately given to the captain, who was then upon deck, and received it with the utmost concern and many bitter oaths. He immediately gave orders to the steersman in favour of the poor thing, as he called it; the sails were instantly slackened, and all hands, as the phrase is, employed to recover the poor animal. I was, I own, extremely surprised at all this; less indeed at the captain's extreme tenderness than at his conceiving any possibility of success; for if puss had had nine thousand instead of nine lives, I concluded they had been all lost. The boatswain, however, had more sanguine hopes, for, having stripped himself of his jacket, breeches, and shirt, he leaped boldly into the water, and to my great astonishment in a few minutes returned to the ship, bearing the motionless animal in his mouth. Nor was this, I observed, a matter of such great difficulty as it appeared to my ignorance, and possibly may seem to that of my fresh-water reader. The kitten was now exposed to air and sun on the deck, where its life, of which it retained no symptoms, was despaired of by all.

The captain's humanity, if I may so call it, did not so totally destroy his philosophy as to make him yield himself up to affliction on this melancholy occasion. Having felt his loss like a man, he resolved to show he could bear it like one; and, having declared he had rather have lost a cask of rum or brandy, betook himself to threshing at backgammon with the Portuguese friar, in which innocent amusement they had passed about two-thirds of their time.

But as I have, perhaps, a little too wantonly endeavoured to raise the tender passions of my readers in this narrative, I should think myself unpardonable if I concluded it without giving them the satisfaction of hearing that the kitten at last recovered, to the great joy of the good captain, but to the great disappointment of some of the sailors, who asserted that the drowning of a cat was the very surest way of raising a favourable wind; a supposition of which, though we have heard several plausible accounts, we will not presume to assign the true original reason.

HENRY FIELDING (1707–54)

In the 5th century BC, the King of Persia ordered his army to attach live cats to the front of their shields when attacking Egypt. The Egyptian soldiers, all cat-worshippers, were loath to wound or kill the cats and so surrendered to the Persians.

'*If animals could speak, the dog would be a blundering outspoken fellow. But the cat would have the rare grace of never saying a word too much.*'
MARK TWAIN

'*Cats are God's way of telling you your furniture is too nice.*'

TO LIVE A CAT AND DOG LIFE
To be always arguing. If not coined by Thomas Carlyle, it was spread abroad by him in his 1858–65 autobiography of Frederick the Great of Prussia: 'There will be jealousies, and a cat-and-dog life over yonder worse than ever.'

THE PATSY AWARD
The American Humane Society created the 'Patsy' award in 1951 in recognition of talented animals appearing in movies. By 1958, the decision was made to include television stars, and 1973 saw the first award for an animal in TV commercials. This was given to a cat named Morris for capturing viewers' attention in advertising catfood. Award-

winners have included Orangey (for his role in the movie *Rhubarb*), Pyewacket (for *Bell, Book and Candle*), Orangey again (for *Breakfast at Tiffany's*), Syn (for *That Darn Cat!*), Midnight (for *Mannix*) and Tonto (for *Harry and Tonto*). Besides cats, the award has also been given to dogs, chimpanzees, dolphins, rats, lions and mules.

'*The smallest feline is a masterpiece.*'
LEONARDO DA VINCI

The cat's tail can convey at least 10 separate signals, expressing what it wishes to communicate at the time, ranging from peaceful relaxation (tail in gentle downward curve, and perked up a bit at the tip), to active aggression against a perceived enemy (tail straight in the air and bristled).

'*If you have Siamese cats you must talk to them a lot.*'
SIR COMPTON MACKENZIE (WHO HAD 11)

TO A LADY

I would be present, aye,
And at my Ladie's call

68

To guard her from the fearfull Mouse,
In Parlour and in Hall;
In Kitchen, for his Lyfe,
He should not shew his head;
The Peare in Poke should lie untoucht
When shee were gone to Bed.
The Mouse should stand in Feare,
So should the squeaking Rat;
And this would I do if I were
Converted to a Cat.

GEORGE TURBERVILLE

'Never feed your cat anything that doesn't match the carpet.'

MORRIS

The large, orange tabby Morris was famous in America between 1969 and 1978 for advertising cat food on television (after he died, similar-looking tabbies replaced him). Several 'quotes' were attributed to Morris, including: 'I don't believe felines are a fad – we're here to stay,' and 'The cat who doesn't act finicky soon loses control over his owner.'

CAT MISCELLANY

'A cat could be man's best friend – but would never stoop to it.'

ANON

FROM *THE HISTORIE OF FOURE-FOOTED BEASTS*, 1607

Cats are of divers colours, but for the most part gryseld... Albertus compareth their eye-sight to carbuncles in darke places, because in the night, they can see perfectly to kill Rattes and Myce...

The tongue of a cat is very attractive, and forcible like a file, attenuating by licking the flesh of a man, for which cause, when she is come neere to the blood, so that her own spittle be mingled therewith, she falleth mad. Her teeth are like a saw, and if the long haires growing about her mouth... be cut away, she looseth hir corage. Her nailes sheathed like the nailes of a Lyon, striking with her forefeete, both Dogs and other things, as a man doth with his hand.

EDWARD TOPSELL

Lord Byron's cat, Beppo, travelled everywhere with him.

'Those who play with cats must expect to be scratched.'

CERVANTES

THE CAT AND MOUSE ACT

After the country of New Zealand allowed all adult women the vote in 1893, and Australia followed suit in 1902, the urge was on worldwide. In Britain, women activists known variously as 'suffragists' or 'suffragettes' took up the cause with energy and diligence. Fearlessly they led public demonstrations to make their voices heard, sometimes destroying property to draw attention to their cause, and frequently breaking the law. The result of this boldness was arrest and often imprisonment. In prison, the suffragists simply refused to eat. The prisons responded by 'force feeding' the unco-operative women, until public outrage brought this to a stop. In 1913 the British Government found a way of dealing with the hunger strikers, by introducing the Prisoner's Temporary Discharge of Ill Health Act. Under this law, women in prison on hunger strike who reached a point of dangerous weakness were discharged. However, they could be rearrested to finish their prison sentence as soon as they regained their health.

The comparison of a powerful government victimising women with a cat 'playing' with a captured mouse quickly resulted in the Prisoner's Temporary Discharge of Ill Health Act becoming known as The Cat and Mouse Act. The expression 'playing cat and mouse' may well have been in use for many years before, but was not attached to a specific law.

Britain allowed all adult women to vote in 1928.

CAT MISCELLANY

*'Cats are poetry in motion – dogs are
gibberish in neutral.'*

*'When a cat sleeps with all four paws tucked
underneath it, cold weather will be coming soon.'*
BRITISH FOLKLORE

> A cut onion rubbed on a no-go surface will
> deter cats, as they dislike the smell. They're
> not keen on vinegar, either – the acidic fumes
> irritate a cat's respiratory system – and the
> crushed leaves of the aromatic rue herb give
> out an aroma that cats hate. Rue has been
> recognised since 1 AD as a repellent to cats.

*'One of the ways in which cats show
happiness is by sleeping.'*
CLEVELAND AMORY

MEHITABEL

This colourful cat character was created by writer
Don Marquis. Mehitabel is convinced that in her
former life she had been Cleopatra. Her current
incarnation, living in the alleys, is rather less grand
than Cleopatra and more than a bit threadbare,
but she is *toujours gai*. Archie the cockroach is her
friend, to whom she utters the slogan 'It's cheerio

my deario that pulls a lady through'. When the adventures of the cockroach and the cat became a Broadway musical in 1957, Mehitabel was played by Eartha Kitt.

'A dog is man's best friend. A cat is cat's best friend.'
ROBERT J VOGEL

In Ancient Egypt cats were worshipped as godly beings. Anyone killing a cat ran the risk of being executed. The death of a family's cat had to be observed by the family going into full mourning and shaving off their eyebrows. The corpse of the humblest pet was not just buried – it was embalmed, mummified and buried with ceremony.

In 1888, a cats' burial ground was uncovered at Beni Hassan in Egypt, and the mummified bodies of thousands of cats were revealed. To the horror of later archaeologists, nearly all the bodies were pulverised to be used as fertiliser in Britain. Only very few genuine mummified cats were kept.

CATERWAUL

This word has been in English use since the 1400s. It means a harsh and strident drawn-out sound, often of a quarrelling nature, like the characteristic cry of cats in heat. The word is echoic, the sound of the word telling you what it means without further consultation. It derives from 'cat' with the addition of an imitative 'yowl'. An old German word – *katerwaulen* – has the same structure and the same meaning, and is also imitative.

Shakespeare was on to it in *Twelfth Night* when Sir Toby and Sir Andrew attempt to sing, and Maria exclaims: 'What a caterwauling do you keep here.'

'When moving to a new house, always put the cat through a window instead of the door. That way it will not leave.'

AMERICAN SUPERSTITION

JAMES BOND

A beautiful white chinchilla cat called Solomon has twice shared the silver screen with Sean Connery: in *You Only Live Twice* (1967) and *Diamonds Are Forever* (1971).

> Cats have few taste receptors on the tongue that respond to sugar, and in general are not interested in sweet things – which benefits their health since their body has a low tolerance to sugar.

'You can't own a cat. The best you can do is be partners.'

SIR HARRY SWANSON

CATGUT

When cats – especially male cats – decide to sing, even the most devoted humans would find it difficult to describe the sounds as lovely music. The same applies when cats are crying in distress.

And there have been times in European history when the sounds of cats being tortured, even burned, were not uncommon. Their noises are believed to be the reason why the strings of musical instruments are identified as coming from cats' intestines, when in fact they do not. As early as the 1600s, comments were made about the sound of inept fiddlers scraping the 'guts of cats' – and, based on the similarity of sound, the likeness had some credibility.

But in fact for centuries musical instruments were customarily fitted with strings made from sheep's intestines, suitably cleaned, treated with certain marinades, dried, stretched and twisted. The result of all this is an impressive cord with great tensile strength and (in the right hands) capable of producing beautiful sounds. Shakespeare gets it right in *Much Ado About Nothing*, when Benedict comments on Balthazar's lute playing: 'Is it not strange that sheep guts should hale souls out of men's bodies.'

Besides making music, the strength of the sheep-gut string was widely used by archers as bowstrings, for hanging the weights of long-case clocks, stitching surgical incisions and to make tennis racquets.

There were two other contributing factors to calling music strings cat-gut. Across Europe in medieval times, powerful superstitions were associated with the killing of cats. During that period, professional string makers (who used sheep) deliberately put about the story that their strings came from cats. It was a ploy to protect their livelihoods, since anybody wanting to set up a rival string business would believe they had to kill cats and therefore face the ominous consequences.

There was also an early German word for a small fiddle – *kitgut*. By misinterpretation in English, it brought about a connotation of cat intestines being associated with violins: not true.

In time, the invention of nylon and finely wound steel made many stringings using traditional 'sheep'-made cords a thing of the past. There is, however, a move back towards the warmer sound that vibrating natural fibre makes.

'Cats know how we feel – they just don't care.'

FROM THE *WIFE OF BATH* (IN THE STYLE OF CHAUCER)

The cat, if you but singe her tabby skin,
The chimney keeps, and sits content within:
But once grown sleek, will from her corner run,
Sport with her tail, and wanton in the sun:
She licks her fair round face, and frisks abroad
To show her fur, and to be catterwaw'd.

ALEXANDER POPE

CAT MISCELLANY

'The cat is domestic only so far as it suits its own ends.'
H H MUNRO

'For the person living alone, nine lives added to one makes a perfect ten.'

MOGGY

The word is usually used affectionately for a cat, but originally it carried a vague feeling that the cat being referred to was of fairly obscure background. Perhaps companionable, but not very sleek or glamorous.

The word has carried that sort of shadow with it for a while. 'Moggy' is a variation on 'Maggie', which for many years was a rather derisive English term for a dishevelled old woman. The term 'maggie' gradually shifted from old crones to cows (presumably because of their similarly inelegant bearing). 'Maggie' slowly changed into 'moggy', still meaning a lumbering cow or a shabby old woman. But, early in the 1900s, when the streets of London abounded with deprived alley cats, the word 'moggy' began to be used to describe these unfortunate creatures. Eventually, the word moved on to cats in general – and it really stuck. 'Moggy' is now widely used to describe not just alley cats, but sometimes also their most elegant cousins.

'There is no need of sculpture in a home which has a cat.'
WESLEY BATES

CATTERY
A place where cats are looked after. The word somehow gives the impression of being contemporary, but has in fact been in use since the late-1700s.

> Cats hiss when they are upset, in danger or to warn off something from their territory. The circumstances in which they hiss are similar to those that provoke a snake. The sounds are also somewhat alike.

'If stretching were wealth, the cat would be rich.'
AFRICAN FOLKLORE

LILITH
The shadowy figure of Lilith – supposed first wife of Adam – was banished from Eden and became forever after associated with images of evil. One version of her story has her becoming a vampiric monster, who liked to disguise herself as a large black cat, and some depictions of her show a woman's face on a cat's body.

FROM *DE RERUM NATURA*, 1398

The catte is a beaste of uncertain heare and colour, for some catte is white, some rede, some black, some skewed and speckled in the fete and in the face and in the eares. And he is in youth swyfte, plyante and mery and lepeth and reseth on all thynge that is tofore him; and is led by a strawe and playeth therewith. And is a right hevy beast in age, and ful slepy, and lieth slily in wait for myce. And he maketh a ruthfull noyse and gustful when one proffereth to fythte with another.

BARTHOLOMEW GLANVIL

'Oh, a cat's a cat. Babou's only too long when he really wants to be. Are we even sure he's black? He's probably white in snowy weather, dark blue at night, and red when he goes to steal strawberries.'

COLETTE

MAD-CAT

Canadian television viewers were introduced to the clumsy, bionic 'Inspector Gadget' in 1983. Through several television series and, later, movies, the Inspector battled against the Malevolent Agency of Destruction and the evil Dr Claw, whose cat was known as MAD-cat.

MAX CRYER

'To a mouse – a cat is a lion.'
ALBANIAN SAYING

THE CAT AND THE FIDDLE

Hey diddle diddle, the cat and the fiddle,
The cow jumped over the moon.
The little dog laughed to see such fun
And the dish ran away with the spoon!

First published in 1765 (as *High Diddle Diddle*),
any explanation of exactly what this song meant
has been lost in the mists of time. One theory is
that it may be the nonsense result of juxtaposing

the goods kept in a poor home: a cat to keep mice under control; a dog to protect the family; a cow for milk; a dish and spoon for the table; and a fiddle for singing and dancing.

'Cats are a mysterious kind of folk. There is more passing in their mind than we are aware of.'
SIR WALTER SCOTT

PUTTING THE CAT AMONG THE PIGEONS

This expression has its origin in unfortunate fact: during the time of the British Raj, soldiers in India between military duties had to find ways of occupying their time. For amusement, sometimes they used to trap wild cats, put them in a caged enclosure with a lot of pigeons, then take bets on how many birds the cat could swipe dead. And so, 'putting the cat among the pigeons' means to cause trouble and make a stir – often by revealing a controversial fact.

CAT AMONG THE PIGEONS

Agatha Christie's 1959 novel *Cat Among the Pigeons* is not about actual cats; the story is a heady mix containing jewels, an exotic prince, nervous schoolgirls – and Hercule Poirot.

> Cats have peripheral vision of 285 degrees.

*'A cat, I am sure, could walk on a
cloud without coming through.'*
JULES VERNE

DR EVIL'S CAT

The *Austin Powers* movies tell us that Dr Evil spent 30 years suspended, frozen, in space. His re-entry to earth went tolerably well – except that his cat was incorrectly thawed and as a result became bald. This plot twist is solved by the role of the cat – Mr Bigglesworth – being played by a hairless Sphynx.

> As busy as a two-headed cat in a creamery.

THE CAT IN THE WELL

Ding, dong, bell, pussy's in the well.
Who put her in? Little Tommy Thin,
Who pulled her out? Little Tommy Stout,
What a naughty boy was that,
To drown poor pussycat.
Who never did him any harm,
But killed the mice in his father's barn!

Versions of this very old rhyme date back to the late 1500s. The song is sometimes seen as a representation of the feudal waifs and wretches who were born to serve their noble lords without question, and died without any appreciation from those they'd served. Others see it as a simple lesson, encouraging children to understand that when an animal has done no harm it is unfair to treat it cruelly.

Shakespeare uses the phrase 'Ding, dong, bell' in *The Merchant of Venice*, Act III:

Let us all ring fancy's bell;
I'll begin it – Ding, dong, bell.
And in *The Tempest*, Act I, Scene II:

Sea nymphs hourly ring his knell:
Hark! Now I hear them – Ding, dong, bell.'

'Most cats, when they are Out want to be In,
and vice versa – often simultaneously.'
LOUIS CAMUTI

GRIN LIKE A CHESHIRE CAT
Alice, of *Alice in Wonderland*, was intrigued when she met a Cheshire cat that could fade into invisibility until only its grin was left. But author

Lewis Carroll didn't invent the expression about the grinning cat; it was known over a century earlier, and is mentioned in Pindar Wolcot's *Works* of 1792. Four centuries before that, a notorious British swordsman called Caterling was nicknamed The Cheshire Cat because he grinned broadly while slaughtering anyone – so a person who grinned widely was sometimes called 'a Cheshire cat'. But, most famously, the cheeses of Cheshire were often made in a circular shape, with a cat's face imprinted on them – and the shape made the cat's face appear to be grinning. So, by 1865, Lewis Carroll had several reasons for making his grinning cat come from Cheshire.

'In order to keep a true perspective of one's importance, everyone should have a dog that will worship him and a cat that will ignore him.'
DEREKE BRUCE

There are over 100 formally recognised breeds of cat, with identifiable characteristics of the breed they claim, and with pedigrees traceable back through several generations. Besides those, any neighbourhood may have other strains of moggy that are not formally recognised; they are certainly cats, but not ones with traceable pedigrees.

FOSS

Writer and artist Edward Lear's cat Foss was partly the source for some of the cats in his nonsense poems, such as *The Owl and the Pussycat*.

'Humans: no fur, no tail, they run away from mice, they never get enough sleep. How can a cat help but love such an absurd animal?'

THE INCREDIBLE JOURNEY

Scottish-born author Sheila Burnford's 1961 novel *Homeward Bound* is an action-adventure about a bull terrier, a Labrador and a Siamese cat. Together they trek 400 kilometres across one of the wildest parts of Canada. It became a Disney movie in 1963 with the new title *The Incredible Journey*. A second movie version appeared in 1993 – this time as 'live action' with the voices of Michael J Fox, Sally Field and Don Ameche providing the 'voices' for the three star animals.

'People who dislike cats will be carried to the cemetery in the rain.'
NETHERLANDS SAYING

SYLVESTER THE CAT

This feline made his debut in a 1945 animated movie cartoon called *Life With Feathers*, then had a follow-up episode *Peck up Your Troubles*. Sylvester quickly established the cry 'suffering succotash!' and in 1947 became an Oscar winner – by which time the character of Tweety Pie the canary had joined the cast. From then on, Sylvester's main aim in life seemed to be to catch Tweety Pie, but through 100 animated cartoons, another Oscar in 1955 and a decade of comic

strips in newspapers, Tweety Pie continued to escape. Besides 'suffering succotash!' the series introduced two other concepts that charmed the public: the Mexican mouse Speedy Gonzales; and the famous song 'I tawt I taw a puddy-tat, a tweeping up on me'. (*Succotash*: a cooked mixture of corn kernels and lima beans.)

> 'Cat's claw' is a vine from the Amazon area, which wraps itself around jungle trees. It has been used for hundreds of years as a medicine for arthritis, gastritis and other illnesses.

'A dog is prose, a cat is a poem.'
JEAN BURDEN

THE CAT AND THE QUEEN

Pussycat, Pussycat where have you been?
I've been to London to look at the Queen.
Pussycat, Pussycat, what did you there?
I frightened a little mouse under a chair.

It is usually believed that the Queen in question was Elizabeth I – whose staff was known to include one courtier with an old cat, which plodded around palaces indiscriminately, and once ventured underneath the Queen's throne when she was sitting on it. Elizabeth was startled, then amused, and announced that the cat had the freedom of the throne room, providing it kept the area free of mice.

'The phrase "domestic cat" is an oxymoron.'
GEORGE F WILL

CAT STEVENS
Cat Stevens was born Steven Demetre Georgiou, of a Greek Cypriot father and Swedish mother. He changed his name in his teenage years to Cat Stevens and enjoyed worldwide success as a singer/songwriter before converting from Greek Orthodox to Muslim. For that he changed his name again, to Yusuf Islam.

ALL CATS ARE GREY IN THE DARK
Not just cats, of course – everything else in the dark is also grey, and so, when the lights are out, appearances are meaningless. But cats in the dark have been the symbol of this concept since the proverb surfaced in 1546: 'When all candels be out – all cats be grey.'

CAT MISCELLANY

*'If cats had wings, there would be no
ducks left in the lake.'*

INDIAN SAYING

SIX LITTLE MICE SAT DOWN TO SPIN

Six little mice sat down to spin
Pussy passed by and she peeped in.
What are you doing, my little men?
Weaving coats for gentlemen.
Shall I come in and cut off your threads?
No, no, Mistress Pussy, you'd bite off our heads.
Oh no, I'll not; I'll help you to spin.
That may be so, but you can't come in.
Says Puss: You look so wondrous wise
I like your whiskers and bright black eyes,
Your house is the nicest house I see
I think there's room for you and me.
The mice were so pleased, they opened the door
And Pussy soon had them all dead on the floor.

ANON

LCS
The Library Cat Society was founded in the US in
1987, and encouraged libraries to have cats in
attendance.

A BAG OF CATS

It doesn't take much effort to imagine the result of putting several cats into one bag. The Irish expression 'bag of cats' refers to any situation which is noisy and bad-tempered; one person in an ugly mood; a gathering which is out of control and turning rebellious; or a political party not noted for its calm behaviour – which is how the term is used in James Joyce's *Dubliners* (1914).

'If you are worthy of its affection, a cat will be your friend, but never your slave.'
THEOPHILE GAUTIER

I'M SO NERVOUS, I'M HAVING KITTENS

A person who is 'having kittens' is in a state of serious upset. But why kittens, and not puppies or baby crocodiles? The expression as it stands dates back to medieval times, when some women were believed to be witches. If a 'witch' had a grievance against another woman, she might cause a spell over the other in her pregnancy, and replace her baby with kittens. Then even the natural pangs of childbirth might be interpreted as the internal clawing of cats' paws, causing dramatic anguish in the labouring woman. Any woman convinced that she was bewitched and about to give birth to a litter of kittens might understandably become hysterical with fright. In later centuries, the use of the term broadened to refer to anyone whose level of calm was being threatened.

'Cats' whiskers are so sensitive they can find their way through the narrowest crack in a broken heart.'

Nature intended cats to be carnivores, and they will become ill on a vegetarian diet.

PUSS IN SPACE
The Cat from Outer Space is a 1978 movie about a UFO, which arrives on earth piloted by a galaxy cat whose special collar enables speech with humans. The cat needs help to return to its cat galaxy, and is assisted by Ken Berry, Sandy Duncan and Roddy McDowall.

'It is better to be a mouse in a cat's mouth – than a man in a lawyer's hands.'
SPANISH SAYING

Australian author Colleen McCullough (*The Thorn Birds*, 1977) lives on Norfolk Island in the Pacific Ocean with her husband – and a cat called Poindexter.

'Dogs look up to us. Cats look down on us. Only pigs treat us as equals.'
WINSTON CHURCHILL

ST IVES

As I was going to St Ives,
I met a man with seven wives;
Every wife had seven sacks;
Every sack had seven cats;
Every cat had seven kits.
Kits, cats, sacks and wives,
How many were there going to St Ives?

Apart from the unlikelihood of a man in England having seven wives all at one time, the verse is a riddle as well as a nursery rhyme – a nonsense song intended to exercise a child's logic rather than their arithmetic skills.

How many were going to St Ives? Why, only one person of course – the others were all *coming away* from St Ives...

'A fortune surely awaits the person who invents mouse-flavoured cat food.'

'WONDERLAND' CAT

Lewis Carroll's *Alice's Adventures in Wonderland* (1865) features a young English girl whose pet cat is called Dinah – although Dinah never actually makes an appearance in the story.

SNAGGLEPUSS

This cat first appeared in cartoons in 1959 as a supporting character, but began in his 'own show' in 1961. Whenever he gets in a fix, which is often, he yells out 'Heavens to Murgatroyd!'. This rapidly became a children's catch-cry among viewers, and is still occasionally heard now as an exclamation of big surprise.

'Cats are smarter than dogs. You'd never get eight cats to pull a sled through the snow.'
JEFF VALDEZ

CATWALK

There is clearly a connection between a cat's ability to negotiate a narrow strip with no side support, and models sashaying along a raised ramp with no rail. But the catwalk isn't a new concept; it has been in use since at least the middle of the 19th century or possibly earlier, when parts of sailing ships were known as catwalks and building sites used the same term for high, narrow communication bridges.

In about 1910 the term started to move into more common usage, especially inside dirigible aircraft. A horizontal ladder-type structure inside the aircraft, on which the crew could move from one area to another, was called a catwalk. Later, the term moved to other aircraft and was used in the Second World War to describe the long plank that stretched between the cockpit and the tail inside bomber aircraft. All these applications were sometimes called 'cat's walk' rather than 'catwalk' – but the 's' was gone by the time the term started to be used in theatre and fashion shows, in about 1950. The words 'ramp' and 'walkway' were also still being used to describe the long narrow platform on which fashion models walked but, by the 1970s, 'catwalk' seemed to have become the universally used term.

CAT BURGLAR

The term has been in use since the early 1900s, and refers to a burglar who can enter premises, steal and depart, without any noticeable noise – like a cat entering and leaving a room. If entry to the property requires adept climbing and some athletics, the similarity to a cat is even more pronounced. In the 1955 movie *To Catch a Thief*, Cary Grant played a retired burglar who had been known as 'The Cat', and Brigitte Auber played a younger and still-active 'cat burglar'.

'I love my cats because I love my home – and little by little they become its visible soul.'
JEAN COCTEAU

THE CAT AND THE PUDDING STRING

Sing, sing, what shall I sing?
The cat's run away with the pudding string!
Do, do, what shall I do?
The cat has bitten it quite in two.
Sing, sing, what shall I sing?
The cat has eaten the pudding string!
Do, do, what shall I do?
The cat's run away with the pudding too.
ANON

*'A rose has thorns, a cat has claws.
Both are worth the risk.'*

CHESHIRE CAT

Lewis Carroll's famous Cheshire Cat explains to Alice that a dog growls when it is angry and wags its tail when it is happy, but that a cat growls when it is happy and wags its tail when it is angry. (Alice doesn't agree that a cat 'growls': 'I call it purring, not growling,' she says.)

> The cat Bastet was supreme goddess of ancient Egypt, and was such a powerful icon that, soon after a human baby was born, it was equipped with a pendant showing her image. Babies' arms were often tattooed in a similar image, which was meant to encourage Bastet to keep watch over the child. From the sacred cats kept in temples, a small amount of blood was often taken and injected into a child – helping to prevent it from catching infectious diseases.

*'Perfect companions never have fewer
than four feet.'*
COLETTE

'A considerate cat will wait until you've read the morning paper before tearing it to shreds.'

*'When the cat of the house is black,
of lovers a lass will not lack.'*
19TH-CENTURY BRITISH BELIEF

During the 1980s, an eccentric cat leaped to prominence in New Zealand. Named Rastus, he developed a taste for riding on his owner's motorbike – and frequently did so, always equipped with helmet and goggles. When an alert tea-packaging company featured the bike-travelling Rastus in television commercials, he rapidly became the subject of a popular song and 10 children's books. Rastus and his owner were both killed in a car crash in 1998, and a nation mourned.

GAY PURREE

The animated movie hit of 1962 tells the story of the country cat Mewsette and her adventures when she comes to the big city. An all-star cast of voices included Judy Garland, Robert Goulet and Hermione Gingold.

RAINING CATS AND DOGS

In Northern European mythology, the gods of nature were believed to be accompanied by animals. Odin, the Scandinavian god of war and master of the winds, was surrounded by wolves and dogs. The ungodly, also – evil spirits and witches – were believed to have been accompanied by cats, and rode on the gusts of storms. According to myth, during strong winds and tumultuous rain, the dogs of wind came out in full cry, chasing away the cats of the evil spirits – who transformed themselves into rain in order to escape. The belief was heightened by the sensation of heavy rain when it hits you, the faint sting like a little scratch, and the sound of thunder – loud, sudden, often several explosions in succession, somewhat like the barking of a huge dog.

The above explanation satisfies most language scholars, but other folk-beliefs have also persisted. In 1653 playwright Richard Brome wrote the line 'It shall rain... dogs and polecats...' (*The City Witt*) – but its meaning was not clear. It has been construed as a reference to the fact that, in old towns, the poor drainage facilities and rudimentary gutters meant that all kinds of filth, moving and still, was exposed to public view. After a big storm, the aforementioned gutter filth could contain the corpses of half-starved stray cats and street-living dogs. Such is described by Jonathan Swift, who wrote of it in 1710: 'Now from all parts the swelling kennels flow, and bear their trophies with them as they go... drowned puppies, stinking sprats, all drenched in mud, dead cats, and turnip-tops, come tumbling down the flood.'

This seems a straightforward description of debris floating in a gutter, without any mention of where the debris originated. Although some believe these once-common events to be a source for the term, it is hardly sufficient to be the provenance of this long-lived expression, even if the more gullible among the citizens believed the bodies in the gutters had fallen from the sky – that it had literally been 'raining cats and dogs'. Presumably the starving street-life animals also died and were seen in the gutters during non-rainy periods. Another dubious source reasons that both cats and dogs tended to live within the thatching of roofs, and literally fell out during heavy rain and wind!

In 1738 – nearly 30 years after his first reference to the puppies and cats in the gutters – Jonathan Swift wrote the phrase in the form we now know it. Some scholars would like to think he was making a connection with the truly ancient mythological belief that connected wind with dogs, and rain with cats. In any case, the expression was in common usage in 19th-century literature.

CAT MISCELLANY

*'The real measure of a day's heat
is the length of a sleeping cat.'*
CHARLES J BRADY

PUSSYFOOT
A hunting cat moves gently and silently on padded feet. Used metaphorically, pussyfooting means to behave in an overly cautious, timid manner and to refrain from saying or doing anything definite. The term seems to have arisen in America late in the 1800s, when a stealthy revenue officer called William E Johnson was given the nickname Pussyfoot. Its wider popularity sprang from its use by US President Theodore Roosevelt in 1903.

WALKS BY HIMSELF
In *The Cat That Walked by Himself*, 1902, Rudyard Kipling agreed that mankind had domesticated dogs, cows and horses, but he pointed out that, although the cat will kill mice and be nice to babies, in between doing that – and especially when it's night and the moon is up – the cat walks alone.

'*When a cat adopts you there is nothing
to be done about it except put up with it
until the wind changes.*'
T S ELIOT

DICK WHITTINGTON'S CAT

A mystery. Though immortalised in a hundred story-books and a thousand pantomime performances, it seems unlikely that Sir Richard Whittington's companion was an actual living, breathing cat. 'Cat' in some contexts means a kind of boat – although the term 'catboat' means different things to different people. Certainly coal from Newcastle was being transported to London even before Whittington became Lord Mayor in 1397, and a catboat was often used for transporting coal. Whittington may have sent such a boat to the King of Barbary and had it return laden with riches. Or, as legend would have it, he may have sent a real cat, which cleaned up the mice in Barbary and earned the King's gratitude. We'll never know, and perhaps it's best we don't. If those who maintain that Dick's 'cat' was in fact a boat were proved right, then many actors would be out of work in the pantomime season, and the London monument to Dick's cat would have to be replaced with a boat, which wouldn't look quite so intriguing.

WHITTINGTON'S CAT STATUE

Even if Dick Whittington had a 'catboat' rather than an actual cat, the legend is powerful enough for there to be a memorial statue of Dick Whittington's cat on Highgate Hill in North London. It is erected on the spot where, reputedly, Whittington heard the bells of Bow church tell him to return to London where he would three times be Mayor.

THE OWL AND THE PUSSYCAT

The Owl and the Pussycat went to sea
In a beautiful pea-green boat.
They took some honey, and plenty of money
Wrapped up in a five-pound note.
The Owl looked up to the stars above,
And sang to a small guitar,
'O lovely Pussy! O Pussy, my love,
What a beautiful Pussy you are,
You are, You are!
What a beautiful Pussy you are!'
Pussy said to Owl, 'You elegant fowl!
How charmingly sweet you sing!
O let us be married! Too long we have tarried:
But what shall we do for a ring?'
They sailed away, for a year and a day,
To the land where the Bong-Tree grows,

And there in a wood a Piggy-wig stood,
With a ring at the end of his nose,
His nose,
His nose!
With a ring at the end of his nose.

'Dear Pig, are you willing to sell for one shilling
Your ring?' said the Piggy, 'I will.'
So they took it away, and were married next day
By the Turkey who lives on the hill.
They dined on mince, and slices of quince,
Which they ate with a runcible spoon;
And hand in hand, on the edge of the sand
They danced by the light of the moon,
The moon,
The moon!
They danced by the light of the moon.

EDWARD LEAR

A totally whimsical and endearing 'nonsense poem' said to have been inspired by Lear's own cat. Part of the poem's charm is its rather ridiculous juxtaposition of images (dining on mince and slices of quince is hardly everyday fare), and the ongoing mystery that is the exact meaning of a 'runcible' spoon. True, someone proposed that it was one of those broad, three-pronged forks commonly used for pickles, but it was only *proposed* – nobody actually knows. There is a possibility that Lear was echoing the old word *rouncival*, which meant large, even gigantic. But it is more than possible that, like the 'Bong-Tree', the author simply invented the word.

'A cat makes all the difference between coming back to an empty house – or coming home.'

TOM AND JERRY

One of the most famous cat-and-mouse pairings in movie cartoons. The cat and mouse originally started out in 1939 being called Jasper and Jinx, when they first appeared in a short Hanna-Barbera cartoon called *Puss Gets The Boot*. In 1941, the pair was recreated by Chuck Jones in *Midnight Snack* with the cat as Tom, in a frenetic pursuit of Jerry the mouse – a pursuit which was maintained for many years. Tom and Jerry continued their chase through 160 movie cartoons, winning seven Oscars. In 1965, their exploits began to be screened on television, and they starred in a full-length animated movie in 1993.

*'The cat is an animal so unpredictable
that you can never tell in advance how it will
ignore you the next time.'*
EVAN ESAR

Ever watchful for customer-pleasing improvements, some parts of the hotel industry have experimented with ways of letting the staff know not to intrude with mop and broom on a still-sleeping inhabitant. The traditional 'Do Not Disturb' sign has been replaced in some establishments by elegantly designed images of 'dreaming' or door-hangers featuring a brief but elegant verse referring to the beauties of sleep.

The door-hanger of one American hotel chain featured no words, just a sketch of a cat napping. Which led to the Riverbend luxury resort in Wisconsin going one step further: each room in the hotel is provided with a stuffed toy cat, stretched out in sleep. Placed outside the door at night, it is an instant message that the 'people indoors' are also asleep. If the toy cat appeals, it can be added to the bill and put into the luggage.

Actor James Mason had a favourite cat called Flower Face.

MRS T TWITCHIT

Beatrix Potter's stories include the charming cat Mrs Tabitha Twitchit and her family, Tom Kitten, Moppett and Mittens.

'When the cat washes itself, then surely we must expect a guest?'
OLD DUTCH SUPERSTITION

THE OWL AND THE PANTHER

I passed by his garden, and marked with
  one eye,
How the Owl and the Panther were sharing
  a pie:
The Panther took pie-crust, and gravy, and
  meat,
While the Owl had the dish as its share of
  the treat.
When the pie was all finished, the Owl, as
  a boon,
Was kindly permitted to pocket the spoon:
While the Panther received knife and fork
  with a growl
And concluded the banquet by ... ...
LEWIS CARROLL

Lewis Carroll's nonsense poem deliberately leaves out the last three words ('eating the owl') – encouraging the listening child to relish the *schadenfreude* of filling them in for his or herself.

'Cats instinctively know the precise moment their owners will waken – then they awaken them ten minutes sooner.'
JIM DAVIS

LUCIFER

Disney's 1950 animated movie *Cinderella* included a cat named Lucifer who belonged to the evil stepmother and her two evil daughters. Not a friendly character, Lucifer behaved with disdain towards poor Cinderella. But, as we all know, one thing led to another and Cinderella finished up with the handsome prince – at which point Lucifer was given a severe comeuppance by Cinderella's dog Bruno.

> Wilberforce, a cat with impressive charisma, lived at 10 Downing Street for over a decade and served four British Prime Ministers. He was officially retired from service in 1987 with a retirement pension approved by Margaret Thatcher. Alas it lasted only one year, as he died in 1988.

SCAREDY CAT OR FRAIDY CAT

These two terms appear to have originated concerning a cat's turn of speed rather than any lack of courage. A cat will hiss, arch, 'puff up' and defy even a sizeable enemy. But, when the same cat recognises genuine danger which bluff won't dissolve, it will escape with alacrity. However, the 'scaredy' and 'fraidy' descriptions referring to timidity have been in use since at least 1900, and appeared in the poem *Moo Cow Moo* by Canadian poet Edmund Cook in 1903.

Cats certainly are not cowards, but they are smart enough to scamper away – often up the nearest tree – when a larger enemy threatens them. This (perfectly sensible) practice has earned them the rather unfair expressions 'fraidy cat' and 'scaredy cat'.

'By and large, people who enjoy teaching animals to roll over will find themselves happier with a dog.'
BARBARA HOLLAND

A CAT HAS NINE LIVES

The myth that cats have nine lives has been around for centuries. In English, it was seen in John Heywood's *Book of Proverbs* in 1546, and soon after in William Baldwin's satirical book *Beware the Cat* (1553): 'It is permitted for a witch to take her cat's body nine times.'

Slightly later, c.1594, Shakespeare mentions it in *Romeo & Juliet*, where Tybalt asks Mercutio: 'What wouldst thou have of me?'

Mercutio replies: 'Good King of Cats, nothing but one of your nine lives.'

The truth is, cats do not have nine lives – they have just one, like every other living creature.

However, cats are particularly good at surviving disasters with the one life they do have. They are small, quick-thinking, lightweight, fast and flexible, and have excellent balance. But the association of cats with nine lives existed in other cultures long before it crept into the English language.

Ancient Egyptians revered the cat, not only because they regarded it as having godlike qualities, but also because it was a practical beast and killed rats. And the Egyptians noticed, of course, that the cat could escape from tricky situations and survive long falls and accidents; therefore they reasoned that it had more lives than just the usual one.

Ancient Egyptians were also keen on numerology, the number three having special significance to them as it still does in many cultures. Furthermore, anything which was a multiple of three was of even greater importance, so they honoured cats by declaring that they possessed 'three times three' lives (in other words, nine). The belief that cats had nine lives inevitably drifted from Egypt elsewhere, and it is mentioned in Indian fables from before Christ and in Arabic fables of similar antiquity.

Of course, the Ancient Egyptians weren't the only people to find significance in certain numbers. The number nine has been a mystical and religious symbol for centuries. The Nordic god Odin gave his female counterpart Freja absolute rule over nine worlds. Some people believe that Jesus died on the cross during the ninth hour.

Even in modern times, the number nine has all sorts of images hovering about it in our consciousness: nine holes of golf; a cat-o'-nine-tails; a game of ninepins; *Deep Space Nine*; nine months of pregnancy; the 'nine levels' of Hell; Cloud Nine; nine major planets; the whole nine yards; dressed to the nines. So it's not surprising that the concept of 'nine lives' has a ring to it, and always did have.

Besides the athleticism of cats, and the various resonances of the figure nine, the belief that cats had nine lives became tangled up with the medieval European belief in witches. From this confusion grew the myth that witches could change themselves into their pet cat a total of nine times. While this concept faded away, the belief (or at least the expression) remains in the English language and the English-speaking psyche that we have only one chance at life – but cats have nine.

'Cats may have nine lives – but they seem to sleep through eight of them.'

AESOP
In 500 BC Aesop, to whom were attributed many Greek fables, generally used animals to make his moral points. A number of his tales concern cats

which, on different occasions, were involved with, an eagle, Venus, a fox, a young mouse, and a cockerel.

'The reason cats climb is so that they can look down on almost every other animal… it's also the reason they hate birds.'
K C BUFFINGTON

TO A CAT

Stately, kindly, lordly friend
Condescend
Here to sit by me, and turn
Glorious eyes that smile and burn,
Golden eyes, love's lustrous meed*
On the golden page I read.

All your wondrous wealth of hair,
Dark and fair,
Silken-shaggy, soft and bright
As the clouds and beams of night,
Pays my reverent hand's caress
Back with friendlier gentleness.

Dogs may fawn on all and some
As they come;

*(*meed* – old word for 'reward')

You, a friend of loftier mind,
Answer friends alone in kind.
Just your foot upon my hand
Softly bids it understand.

ALGERNON CHARLES SWINBURNE

'Cats can work out mathematically the exact place to sit which will cause the most inconvenience.'

PAM BROWN

'Definition of a cat toy: Anything not nailed down.'

> Theatre productions of the musical *Cats* used standard condoms to protect the body microphones worn by the cast.

THE CAT'S PYJAMAS

During the 1920s, a wide collection of bizarre 'approval' expressions arose by attaching nonsense attributes to animals: the eel's ankle; the oyster's garter; the snake's hips; the canary's tusks; the flea's eyebrows; the sardine's whiskers; the kipper's knickers; the elephant's instep; the bee's knees; and *the cat's pyjamas*.

The terms were not intended to be taken seriously; they are simply exclamations praising something of rare quality – outstanding and to be admired. Of all these absurd expressions, the cat's pyjamas may have been one whose basis lay in fact. It is believed (but not proven) that during the late 1700s there was a London tailor called E B Katz who specialised in making luxurious silk garments – including pyjamas – for royalty and other wealthy patrons.

But some writers believe that both 'the cat's pyjamas' and 'the cat's meow' originated in American girls' schools around the beginning of the 20th century. Putting aside the exact origin of the expression, there certainly is evidence for how the term 'cat's pyjamas' became widely popularised. Tad Dorgan, an American sportswriter and cartoonist, used the phrase freely and is credited with bringing it to a wider public. (He is also credited with either inventing or popularising the term 'hot dog'.)

*'Cats have an infallible understanding
of total concentration – and how to get
between you and it.'*
ARTHUR BRIDGES

116

SNOWBALL

In *The Simpsons*, the famous yellow family lost their cat, Snowball, in a car accident. Their daughter Lisa wrote an emotional poem about their beloved pet:

> *Meditations on Turning Eight*
> I had a cat named Snowball
> She died! She died!
> Mom said she was sleeping
> She lied! She lied!
> Why oh why is my cat dead?
> Couldn't that Chrysler hit me instead!

The moggy was replaced by Snowball II.

THE CAT IN THE HAT

Theodore Geisel was a cartoonist and creator of advertising campaigns when a 1954 survey of schoolchildren in America revealed that literacy standards were falling. The children found their required reading books boring. Together with a publisher, Geisel compiled a list of 250 words considered 'important' to help children learn reading, and then Geisel set out to make a story out of those words and to illustrate it.

The result, in 1957, was *The Cat in The Hat*, published under Geisel's pen-name Dr Seuss. Ever since, the book has been among the Top 10 best-selling hardcover books for children.

CAT MISCELLANY

'It is better to feed one cat than many mice.'
NORWEGIAN SAYING

CRUEL, BUT COMPOSED AND BLAND

Cruel, but composed and bland,
Dumb, inscrutable and grand,
So Tiberius might have sat,
Had Tiberius been a cat.

MATTHEW ARNOLD

FAT CAT

This term is used to describe a rich and influential person, while suggesting associated imagery of self-importance, self-indulgence and probable laziness.

This may not be entirely fair, since a real cat could have become fat because it has been well loved and cared for. Nevertheless, contributors of revenue to American political groups during the 1920s became known as 'fat cats', and in 1928 the term was widely popularised by Frank Kent, a writer on the Baltimore *Sun*, who used it in his book *Political Behaviour*. Since then the expression has broadened its application and also increased in its 'put-down' quality. Besides politicians and their rich supporters, it is now often

118

applied to business people and administrators who are perceived as taking the 'cream' and disadvantaging the workers.

THE ARISTOCATS

An animated Disney movie from 1970. Eva Gabor provided the voice for Duchess, the star character. Set in Paris, 1910, the story tells of how Duchess, a beautiful pedigree cat, is kidnapped to prevent her from coming into a cat fortune. The rough alley-cat Scat was voiced by Scatman Crothers.

The 'Scottish fold' is the result of an aberration, which was then continued by careful breeding. The cats' ears curl over on to their head and look 'folded'.

'The clever cat eats cheese and breathes down rat holes with baited breath.'

W C FIELDS

TO SIT IN THE CATBIRD SEAT

Catbirds, which are related to mocking-birds, live in America, and like their relatives are capable of a wide variety of imitative sounds – including a credible mimic of a mewing cat, hence their name. Apparently, the catbird likes to sing while perched as high up as possible from the ground – safe from enemies and also commanding a fine view. From this arose the image of the 'catbird seat' as being in an advantageous place, and so the expression began to be used first by American poker players, then by sports broadcasters to describe a player who appeared to be in a particularly fortunate situation. In 1942, a mention of the phrase by American humorist James Thurber in a short story put the phrase into greater prominence. Today, the application of 'in the catbird seat' seems to imply a position of ease, with or without having actual advantages.

'A kitten is so flexible that she is almost double;
the hind parts are equivalent to another kitten –
with which the forepart plays. She does not
discover that the hind part belongs to
her until you tread on it.'
HENRY DAVID THOREAU

LADY AND THE TRAMP
Made in 1955, this Disney production was the
first animated feature film in Cinemascope. It told
of a gentle spaniel, Lady, who fell in with a rough
lot – among whom were two mean Siamese cats
called Si and Am. Peggy Lee provided voices for
both Si and Am.

'Cat names are for human benefit –
they give one a certain degree more confidence
that the animal belongs to you.'
ALAN AYCKBOURN

THERE WAS AN OLD BULLDOG
NAMED CAESAR

There was an old bulldog named Caesar
Who went for a cat, just to tease her

But she spat and she spit
Till the poor bulldog quit
Now when poor Caesar sees her, he flees her.

ANON

CAT'S PAW

Apart from the literal meaning, the term 'cat's paw' is taken as a put-down by a person who has been used by someone else to do his or her donkey-work. In other words a dupe, a pawn, a sucker. The expression dates back to a distant fable about a wily monkey watching some chestnuts roasting in embers. Although the chestnuts reached perfect roasted readiness, the monkey was unwilling to retrieve them and risk his own paws in the heat. So he waylaid a passing cat, and asked it to draw the chestnuts from their red-hot bed. Uncharacteristically agreeable (and stupid) the cat obliged, receiving burned paws for its trouble while the monkey enjoyed the nuts!

So we have the image of a person facing a foolish or even dangerous situation, which they want turned to their advantage, and then organising that the dirty work be done by someone else who thinks they're being helpful – a cat's paw.

> Writer Thomas Carlyle (1795–1881) had a cat named Columbine.

'To err is human; to purr is feline.'
ROBERT BYRNE

'Cats demonstrate total clarity of judgement and taste – the best of anything can be deemed as just satisfactory.'

CATTY-CORNER

The term is widely used in America to mean 'diagonal' but, when asked, most people are flummoxed as to what the connection is between cats and a diagonal corner. The answer is, there is no connection. 'Catty-corner' has nothing to do with cats.

The expression is derived from the French word 'quatre' meaning 'four'. In the Southern states of the US, this French word developed a dialect pronunciation (and spelling) and became 'cater' – so 'cater-cornered' meant simply 'four-cornered' – first seen in the 1880s. It could have stayed like that – but a custom arose whereby a diagonal position was described as 'cater-corner across'. Shortened to 'cater-corner', it underwent a further subtle change because its sound reminded people of cats, and the word became 'catty-corner', or sometimes 'kitty-corner'. But only in America – saying it elsewhere would get nothing but a puzzled reaction.

TONTO

A hit movie in 1974, *Harry and Tonto* was the tale of an elderly widower (Art Carney) whose apartment was demolished for a parking lot. He set out across America accompanied by his cat Tonto. On the way, they gain a young woman companion and, when the trio reaches California, the young woman settles down with Harry's grandson.

'*A cat is a lion in her own lair.*'
INDIAN PROVERB

SAID A MISERLY LORD AT THE ABBEY

Said a miserly lord at the Abbey
'I fear I shall look rather shabby
For I've replaced my ermine,
Infested with vermin,
With the fur of my dear defunct tabby.'
ANON

POE'S *BLACK CAT*

Edgar Allan Poe's horrifying short story *The Black Cat* (1843) dispels any belief held by pragmatists that cats cannot possibly have mystic powers.

BLACK CATS

Black cats were popular long before they became associated with black magic, witches and sorcery. But, once these beliefs took hold, black cats were outlawed by the Christian church. However, only the completely black cats qualified as servants of the devil; any cat with the slightest touch of white on its coat was considered as not entirely belonging to Old Nick. The slaughter of all-black cats caused them to become quite rare, and even today a tiny patch or sprinkling of white on an otherwise black cat is a reminder that this 'imperfection' was once vital to the creature's survival.

Author Mark Twain possessed cats with the names Blatherskite, Zoroaster, Sin, Satan, Tammany, Apollinaris and Sour Mash.

'Cat rule Number 1: When in doubt... wash.'
PAUL GALLICO

CATCALLS

When Samuel Pepys wrote in his 1659 diary that he had bought a 'catcall', he was referring to a kind of whistle used at public performances to express disapproval. Theatre patrons who didn't have such a whistle would imitate the sound of it by making wauling noises like the cries of a cat. In the theatre today, to make catcalls can still express scorn.

CATERPILLAR

In ancient French, the caterpillar was known as 'chatepelose', meaning 'hairy cat'. It's likely that a version of the Old French word was transferred to English – where the original word for caterpillar was 'catyrpel', first seen in print in 1440. But two other English words influenced the final form. 'Cater' has the sense of 'providing food', and the old form of 'pill' was used to mean 'plunder' (surviving in the modern word 'pillage'). It's well known that caterpillars in full feast can plunder the local greenery. By 1775, when Dr Johnson published his famous dictionary, the spelling had settled into 'caterpillar'. In the meantime, the French had modified their ancient word 'chatepelose' to the more contemporary word 'chenille' – a curious switch in imagery, considering the word for 'hairy cat' has become a word derived from the Latin for 'little dog'!

'If cats could talk, they wouldn't.'
NAN PORTER

GARFIELD

The first *Garfield* cartoon was published on 19 July 1979. Since then, the cat's philosophy has been compared to that of Nietzsche, Aristotle, Descartes and Jean-Paul Sartre. He had his first TV special in 1982, followed by nine other Garfield 'themed' television specials involving Christmas, Halloween, Hollywood and Paradise. He starred in his first full-length movie in 2004. A recently developed breed of marigold is named after the lasagne-loving cat – because it is the same colour as Garfield!

ARLENE

Garfield's girlfriend. No shrinking violet, Arlene argues with Garfield about his need to go on a diet, and agonises about her own wish to have her teeth fixed. Circling around their lives is young Nermal, the self-proclaimed 'World's cutest kitten'. Garfield finds the kitten's conceit and self-confidence highly irritating.

CAT MISCELLANY

'If the farm cat's skittish, the farmer's wife is shrewish.'
SCANDINAVIAN SAYING

SONNET TO A CAT

Cat! who hast pass'd thy grand cliacteric*,
How many mice and rats hast in thy days
Destroy'd? – How many tit bits stolen? Gaze
With those bright languid segments green,
    and prick
Those velvet ears – but pr'ythee do not stick
Thy latent talons in me – and upraise
Thy gentle mew – and tell me all thy frays
Of fish and mice, and rats and tender chick.
Nay, look not down, nor lick thy dainty
    wrists –
For all the wheezy asthma, – and for all
Thy tail's tip is nick'd off – and though
    the fists
Of many a maid have given thee many
    a mail,
Still is that fur as soft as when the lists
In youth thou enter'dst on glass bottled wall.
JOHN KEATS

---

*cliacteric – possibly an archaic variant on 'climateric': 'a critical period in life, usually indicating the beginning of decline'.

'Cat mantra: "Sleep and eat, eat and sleep, sleep and eat – is there no end to this overwork?"'

A cat's ability to detect smells is 12 times more efficient than that of humans. The humblest moggy possesses over 60 million olfactory cells.

THE KITTY

The pool of money paid in by participants in a common activity, the whole being used as winnings. There are two schools of thought about why it is called 'the kitty'.

One version links the expression to the old French card game of *faro*. The patron image of *faro* was a tiger – possibly because tiger images were frequently associated with Chinese gambling houses. Reputedly, a picture of a tiger was also hung outside venues where *faro* was being played. Gradually, the accumulated betting money took on the name of the tiger image, and over time was jocularly referred to as 'the kitty'. Not only did the name stick, but also the use of it widened beyond *faro* into other card games and activities involving pool money. To add to this money was 'to sweeten (or fatten) the kitty'.

However, diligent language students trace a connection between 'the kitty', in its sense of 'an accumulating pile of money', back to an old British dialect word, 'kidcot'. The word literally meant 'a place where young goats were kept', but came to be a slang term for prison. 'Kidcot' developed into 'kitcot' and eventually 'kitty', and was attached to the money pool in card games because the word had somehow developed a shade of meaning implying isolation and protection. Such protection was needed for the desired pool of money, which could not be 'released' until someone won.

One more – perhaps tenuous – theory behind the origin of the word 'kitty' is connected with the game of lawn bowls. In bowls, one white ball is stationary and players roll their own bowling balls as close as possible to it, if possible knocking any opponents' bowls out of the way. We don't know what Sir Francis Drake called that ball when he was famously playing bowls in 1588, but he might have called it a 'kitty', a name widely used for this ball nowadays. But the reason for naming that ball 'kitty' has been lost in the mists of time. One possibility has emerged: that the white ball, which is also known as the 'jack', took on a more feminine name when women took part in the game. It therefore became the 'jack' for men and the 'kitty' for women. But, if this story is true, the line has become very blurred (the ball is also known as the 'sweetie', the 'bill' or also – sometimes – the 'cat'!).

DUFF
In the 1977 movie *The Late Show*, a cat named Duff is central to the action. When the cat is stolen from its owner (Lily Tomlin), the attempt to rescue it results in the death of the partner of a detective (Art Carney), who vows to find the murderer.

KITTY

This word is often perceived as connected to 'cat', though there seems no obvious connection between the two words. Nevertheless, the two words are frequently used interchangeably. 'Kitty' may be a slight alteration of the Turkish word *kedi*, meaning *cat*. As a diminutive of 'kitten' it is also used, particularly as an affectionate term for a cat, and especially when calling it to approach. 'Kitten' comes from the Middle English word 'kitoun'.

'A cat's rage is beautiful, burning with pure cat flame, all its hair standing up and crackling blue sparks, eyes blazing and sputtering.'
WILLIAM S BURROUGHS

TRAINED CATS

In the previously considered impossible task of training cats, Japanese animal trainer Satoru Tsuda was a highly successful pioneer. In order for cats to appear in television commercials, he taught them to hold poses, stand on their hind legs and keep 'clothes' on. They appeared as Samurai warriors, street hoodlums, rock musicians, police officers, schoolteachers and pupils. Satoru Tsuda became rich – and took care that his cats were fed and looked after accordingly.

'I had been told that the training procedure with cats was difficult. It's not. Mine had me trained in two days.'

BILL DANA

OSCAR WILDE, ON UNDERSTANDING THE CAT

Poets, I believe, are more closely in touch with the spirit of grimalkin, the soul of a pussycat, than either prose writers or painters. They should be, because poets are mystics, at least the great poets are mystics, speaking like the oracle or the clairvoyant, words that come, of which they themselves may not even understand the meaning. And the poet knocks at gates which sometimes open wide, disclosing gardens to which entrance is denied to those who stumble to find truth in reason and experience. Faith is needed to comprehend the cat, to understand that one can never completely comprehend the cat.

The Silent Meow is a book 'written' by a cat and translated by Paul Gallico. It gives advice on property rights, food, behaviour and protocol.

FELIX THE CAT

Felix was a cartoon character with a truly phenomenal impact. His life began in 1919 when he was created by American artist Otto Messmer, and first seen in an animated movie short called *Feline Follies*. His name, Felix, was contrived as a combination of 'feline' and 'felicity' – which, since it meant 'happiness', was seen as an antidote to any lingering suspicious concern about black cats. Such was Felix's success that within 10 years he had appeared in 150 animated cartoons. His newspaper comic-strip debut in 1923 led to his appearance in over 200 publications worldwide, in many languages.

Felix's popularity grew enormously and, besides featuring on a proliferation of toys, games, cards and jewellery, he featured on the first balloon in the Macy's Thanksgiving Parade and was the mascot chosen by Charles Lindbergh on his famous flight across the Atlantic. A 'Felix doll' was used in early American television experiments, and Felix became the first image to be transmitted by NBC television.

Over 200 episodes of Felix's adventures were shown and repeated on American television in 20 years. A full-length *Felix the Cat, the Movie* played in rotation on the Disney Channel for 10 years, and nine million 'Felix meals for kids' were sold in Wendy's fast-food chain.

In the 21st century, Felix began an even greater

popularity in Japan with a new television series and the creation of a Japanese theatre musical. The early classic cartoons have been released on DVD and enthusiastic celebrity fans include Ringo Starr, Whoopie Goldberg, Justin Timberlake, Cameron Diaz and the Dixie Chicks, while fashion publications featuring Felix include *Vogue*, *Cosmopolitan* and *Elle*. Another movie, *Felix Saves Christmas*, has been released, and plans exist for at least three more.

'*I am as vigilant as a cat to steal cream.*'
FALSTAFF, FROM SHAKESPEARE'S
HENRY IV PART ONE

CATS AND DOGS
In the 1880s, 'cats and dogs' was an American slang term on the stock market, referring to speculative stocks and shares of doubtful value or suspicious history.

'*Dogs eat. Cats dine.*'
ANN TAYLOR

HEP CATS

During the era of slave trading, many black slaves shipped to America took the African language of Wolof with them. Later generations of black Americans who called a man a 'cat' are believed to have been using a derivative of the Wolof word 'kai', meaning 'person.' During the early and mid-20th century, another Wolof word rose to prominence: 'hipi'. In its home country, 'hipi' means 'to be awake and aware; to be alive to what's going on'. From this expression we got people who were 'hip' or 'hep', some of whom became 'hepcats', while others became 'hippies'.

'A kitten in the animal word is what a rosebud is in the garden.'
ROBERT SOUTHEY

SEX KITTEN

The term 'sex symbol' has been in use since about 1910. But in 1956, when 22-year-old French actress Brigitte Bardot burst on to the screen in *And God Created Woman*, a variation in the expression arose: 'sex kitten'. Worldwide, real kittens refrained from comment.

'My sister crying, our maid howling,
our cat wringing her hands!'
LAUNCE, FROM SHAKESPEARE'S
TWO GENTLEMEN OF VERONA

THE CAT OF CATS

I am the cat of cats. I am
The everlasting cat.
Cunning, and old, and sleek as jam,
The everlasting cat.
I hunt the vermin in the night
The everlasting cat –
For I see best without the light –
The everlasting cat.

WILLIAM BRIGHTY RANDS

'Some men there are that love not a gaping pig!
Some that are mad when they behold a cat!'
SHYLOCK, FROM SHAKESPEARE'S MERCHANT OF
VENICE ACT IV, SCENE I

TO FIGHT LIKE KILKENNY CATS
To engage in a battle that neither party can win, and
in which the parties end up destroying each other.

There is no substantial reason for believing that cats in the Irish county of Kilkenny are any more bellicose or aggressive than cats anywhere else. But at least two legends persist in trying to convince us that the cats of Kilkenny are lightweight champions of the world.

The allusion can be dated back to 1798 – a rebellious year in Ireland when foreign soldiers were garrisoned there. Bored with guard duties, it is believed that the soldiers would tie two cats together by their tails, then throw them into a 'fighting area' and watch the (very lively) battle. An addition to the basic story is that one day, as one of these fights was going on, an officer was spied approaching. A quick-thinking soldier drew his sword, severed the two tails letting the cats escape, and told the officer the cats had eaten each other and left only their tails!

But, setting aside the sadistic soldiers, the fighting 'cats' may be a reference to fighting men. During the 17th century, the residents of Irishtown and Kilkenny had a bitter argument over the boundaries, and their persistent battling was compared to the fighting of cats.

There is no proof to either of the stories, but nevertheless the cats of Kilkenny have been left with a reputation for fighting with complete determination right to the bitter end, in an all-out conflict where no one can win.

A folk poem helps keep the belief alive:

There once were two cats from Kilkenny,
Each thought there was one cat too many,
They fought and they fit,
And they scratched and they bit,
Till excepting their nails,
And the tips of their tails,
Instead of two cats,
There weren't any.

THE CAT'S MEOW

With this movie of 2001 it was remarkably difficult to work out the relevance of the title to the semi-factual story, which was about the mysterious death of a Hollywood millionaire while on a leisure cruise in William Randolph Hearst's private yacht. Where does a cat come in that story? Ah! 'Cat's Meow' was the name of the luxury boat on which they were sailing...

'My cat does not talk as respectfully to me as I do to her.'
COLETTE

THE CAT CAME BACK

Old Mister Johnson had troubles of his own
He had a yellow cat which wouldn't leave
   its home;
He tried and he tried to give the cat away,
He gave it to a man goin' far, far away.

But the cat came back the very next day,
The cat came back, we thought he was a goner
But the cat came back; it just couldn't stay
   away.

The cat it had some company one night out in
   the yard,

Someone threw a boot-jack, and they threw it
    mighty hard;
It caught the cat behind the ear, she thought it
    rather slight,
When along came a brick-bat and knocked
    the cat out of sight

But the cat came back... etc.

The man around the corner swore he'd kill
    the cat on sight,
He loaded up his shotgun with nails
    and dynamite;
He waited and he waited for the cat to come
    around,
Ninety-seven pieces of the man is all
    they found.

But the cat came back... etc.

He gave it to a little boy with a dollar note,
Told him for to take it up the river in a boat;
They tied a rope around its neck, it must have
    weighed a pound
Now they drag the river for a little boy
    that's drowned.

But the cat came back... etc.

He gave it to a man going up in a balloon,

He told him for to take it to the man in
the moon;
The balloon came down about ninety
miles away,
Where he is now, well I dare not say.

But the cat came back... etc.

He gave it to a man going way out West,
Told him for to take it to the one he loved
the best;
First the train hit the curve, then it jumped
the rail,
Not a soul was left behind to tell the
gruesome tale.
But the cat came back... etc.

On a telegraph wire, sparrows sitting in
a bunch,
The cat was feeling hungry, thought she'd
like 'em for a lunch;
Climbing softly up the pole, and when
she reached the top,
Put her foot upon the electric wire, which tied
her in a knot.

But the cat came back... etc.

While the cat lay and sleeping and resting
one day

Around came an organ grinder and he began
    to play
The cat looked around awhile, and kinda
    raised her head
When he played *Ta-rah-rah-boom-dee-ay* the
    cat just fell dead.

But its ghost came back the very next day,
Yes, its ghost came back, maybe you will
    doubt it,
But its ghost came back; it just couldn't
    stay away.

HARRY S MILLER (1893)

America issued official postage stamps
featuring cats in 1988. They were by no means
the first nation to do so: cats and cat folklore
have been featured on the official postage
stamps of Germany, Panama, Hungary,
Poland, Colombia, Monaco and Paraguay.

*'After scolding one's cat, one looks into its
face and is seized by the ugly suspicion that it
understood every word. And has filed it
for future reference.'*
CHARLOTTE GRAY

'I purr, therefore I am.'

Various explanations have been put forward as to *how* cats purr. No one explanation agrees with any of the others, so they should perhaps be called 'speculations'. Nobody knows for sure how a cat purrs.

FROM *THE HISTORIE OF FOURE-FOOTED BEASTS*, 1607

The nature of this Beast is, to love the place of her breeding, neither will she tarry in any strange place... most contrary to the nature of a Dogge, who will travaile abroad with his maister... Those which will keepe their Cattes within doores... must cut off their ears, for they cannot endure to have drops of raine distil into them... It is a neate and cleanely creature...They love fire and warme places... They desire to lie softe.

EDWARD TOPSELL

'I hear the cats dreaming of scraps.'
A PUNJAB WAY OF SAYING SOMEONE IS RUMBLING
WITH HUNGER

JOSIE AND THE PUSSYCATS

This 2001 movie had nothing to do with real cats – its story was about an all-woman rock band with a provocative name.

WHEN THE CAT'S AWAY, THE MICE WILL PLAY

Without supervision, some people misbehave. The Romans knew it as 'Dum felis dormit, mus gaudet et exsilit antro' ('When the cat falls asleep, the mouse comes out of its niche'). The saying drifted into French as 'Où chat na rat regne' ('Where there is no cat, the rat reigns'), and featured in the English language in the 1500s in various forms, such as in John Florio's *Firste Frutes*: 'When the cat is abroade the mise will play'.

The proverb turns up in Shakespeare's *Henry V* (1599) when Westmoreland speaks of 'playing the mouse in absence of the cat'. By the time Thomas Heywood wrote *A Woman Killed with Kindness* (printed 1607) he referred to it as 'an old proverb'. The Scottish version has a particular charm: 'Well kens the mouse when the cat is out of the house'.

'The cat is a dilettante in fur.'
THEOPHILE GAUTIER

CAT'S BRAINS

This doesn't refer to the moggy intellect; it's the name geologists give to a mixture found in nature, of sandstone with chalk veins.

WALK THE CAT BACK (OR WALK BACK THE CAT)

Not a commonly used expression, but it surfaced in the US during the 1980s. It means to cast the mind back and assemble a sequence of events that led to a particular situation, and then analyse the initial reasons why the events happened and what they have led to. The term came to prominence in the *New York Times Magazine* during the 1994 investigations into CIA activities.

'Definition of a catacomb: A device used for brushing the cat.'

British humorist Edward Lear at one time had a new house built. The builders were instructed to make the new dwelling an exact copy of the old one – so that the family cat would not be confused when they eventually took up residence.

'They'll take suggestion as a cat laps milk.'
ANTONIO, FROM SHAKESPEARE'S
THE TEMPEST ACT II

A DOG WILL OFTEN STEAL A BONE

A dog will often steal a bone
But conscience lets him not alone,
And by his tail his guilt is known.
But cats consider theft as game
And, howsoever you may blame,
Refuse the slightest sign of shame.

ANON

Actress Janet Leigh called her cat Turkey.

'A cat is a puzzle for which there is no solution.'
HAZEL NICHOLSON

NERVOUS AS A CAT IN A ROOM FULL OF ROCKING CHAIRS

Like any other creature, cats don't like danger from an unpredictable source. It is not very likely that a room ever would be full of rocking chairs. But, if it were, there's no doubt a cat would be uncomfortable for two reasons. Being on the chair seat would give a feeling of being unbalanced and no longer in control. Then, attempting to find a path across the floor, the cat might – heaven forbid – be gazumped on the tail or elsewhere by a rampant, plunging rocker. So, although it might seldom happen in real life, this quaint expression summons an immediate image of worry, jumpiness and inability to relax.

DENNIS THE MENACE
In 1976, Hank Ketcham's cartoon creation Dennis the Menace told his mother: '"Meow" is like "Aloha" – it can mean anything!'

ON THE DEATH OF A CAT

Who shall tell the lady's grief
When her Cat was past relief?
Who shall number the hot tears
Shed o'er her, belov'd for years?
Who shall say the dark dismay
Which her dying caused that day?

MAX CRYER

Come, ye Muses, one and all,
Come obedient to my call.

Of a noble race she came,
And Grimalkin was her name
Young and old fully many a mouse
Felt the prowess of her house;
Weak and strong fully many a rat
Cowered beneath her crushing pat;
And the birds around the place
Shrank from her too close embrace.

But one night, reft of her strength,
She lay down and died at length;
Spare her line and lineage,
Guard her kitten's tender age,
And whoever passes by
The poor grave where Puss doth lie,
Softly, softly let him tread,
Nor disturb her narrow bed.

(ABRIDGED) CHRISTINA ROSSETTI

DO IT IN A CAT'S PAW

Again referring to the gentle (and often silent) ways in which a cat can go about its business. To 'do it in a cat's paw' means to perform some project so discreetly that nobody is aware it is being done.

'Any cat who misses a mouse pretends it was aiming for a dead leaf.'
CHARLOTTE GRAY

POLECAT

'Polecat' is a complete misnomer because the animal has nothing to do with cats or poles. Its name arose from the Continental version of the creature being called in French a 'poule chat' – a cat that stole hens. Because thefts took place only at night, there was confusion about what animal was actually doing the deed – and cats were blamed. The English version of the name was used to describe British ferrets (very slightly different from their Continental cousins), and it stuck.

While the polecat/ferret is often considered to be a less-than-loveable mammal, there have been periods in fashion when its fur was very desirable indeed. The ferret's fur was known as 'fitch', and is a close cousin to mink and ermine.

'Caterpillar: A carpeted post for cats to scratch against.'

'If your cat falls out of a tree, go indoors to laugh.'
PATRICIA HITCHCOCK

Why are cats sometimes associated with women? The interest generated by Egypt's goddess Bast (a female goddess with a cat head) lives with us still. Bast was goddess of motherhood, fertility, happiness and pleasure. Those factors sit easily with cats: they are normally good mothers, find luxury hard to resist, are adept at finding warmth and comfort and, above all, epitomise beauty and graceful movement. Throughout history the same characteristics have been manifested by women.

> Los Angeles soprano Mary O'Brien had a favourite cat of eccentric temperament, called Dumbcluck.

'WHAT'S NEW PUSSYCAT?'
Tom Jones's big hit in 1965. The song, composed by Burt Bacharach and Hal David, had little to do with cats – though it was described by one reviewer as 'an anthem for Las Vegas hepcats'. It was sung with Jones's usual impact and gusto as the title for a movie of the same name, starring Peter O'Toole and written by Woody Allen.

CAT MISCELLANY

'The man who doesn't love cats will never have a pretty woman.'
<small>DUTCH PROVERB</small>

> A truly devoted (but dumb) cat lover thought an 'octopus' meant 'eight cats'.

SHE SIGHTS A BIRD

She sights a bird – she chuckles –
She flattens – then she crawls –
She runs without the look of feet
Her eyes increase to balls –

Her jaws stir – twitching – hungry –
Her teeth can hardly stand –
She leaps, but Robin leaped the first –
Ah, Pussy of the sand,

The hopes so juicy ripening –
You almost bathed your tongue –
When Bliss disclosed a hundred toes –
And fled with every one.

<small>EMILY DICKINSON</small>

'A cat's worst enemy is a closed door.'

CATNAP

A fairly obvious derivation, because cats' ability to sleep is legendary, but the 'catnap' is characterised by two factors: it is brief (rather than being a long, luxurious sleep) and it involves 'dozing lightly' rather than sleeping deeply. Like a cat, a person catnapping can come back to life fairly promptly. It is believed that the faculty of hearing is still active in a catnapping cat.

'A black cat crossing your path signifies that the animal is going somewhere.'
GROUCHO MARX

CATNIP

The plant *Nepeta cataria* is a relative of ordinary mint and, like mint, is pleasantly aromatic. But this species has an oil called *hepetalactone* whose particular aromatic quality might not enhance the flavour of green peas, but certainly gives cats a few minutes of pleasure. They will first sniff at the plant, then tackle it with their teeth and tongue, and rub their fur against it. The result: moderate but uninhibited ecstasy, after which, normal behaviour is quickly resumed as if nothing had ever happened. (Valerian has a similar effect.)

153

Especially devoted cat-owners can buy 'essence of catnip' in a spray-can, and use it to make a cat's toys or scratch-post more exciting.

FIGARO
In 1883, Italian writer Carlo Lorenzini (aka Collodi) created the story of Pinocchio and Geppetto (who did not have a pet cat). Over 50 years later, the story was made into a wildly successful Disney movie (1940). But purists were not pleased, as the movie added two 'characters' that didn't exist in the original story: Cleo the goldfish and Figaro the (very charming) cat.

SEE WHICH WAY THE CAT JUMPS
Both the English and French have the saying 'See which way the wind blows' (*Voir d'où vient le vent*) – meaning to wait until various factors fall into place before making a decision. Transferring the notion to cats is entirely logical, since cats can be very unpredictable. The transition from 'wind blowing' to 'cat jumping' was established by the 19th century, and you can find it in the *Universal Songster* of 1825:

> He soon saw which way the cat did jump,
> And his company he offered plump.

But the entry of the 'cat jumps' phrase into the English language has a cruel history. In the days when cats were considered totally expendable, their unpredictability was seen as an asset by sportsmen and marksmen practising their skills. In a game called 'tip-cat', the unfortunate creature would be placed up a small tree, or on top of a medium-height pole. The sportsman was not permitted to shoot the cat while static on its perch, but only in motion. Some would align themselves to shoot where they thought the cat would jump – often without success. The smart operator, confident of his speedy aim and quick trigger, would wait to *see which way the cat jumped*, and

then aim and fire while the cat was in mid-air. From this activity came the image of waiting until a situation had progressed to the point where action would be advantageous – such as sharemarket investors, who interpret a buying or selling trend before acting on it themselves, and therefore wait to 'see which way the cat jumps'.

AILUROPHILE

A person who loves cats. The word arises from the Greek word for cat, *ailorus* – strictly meaning 'the waving one' and based on a reference to the cat's tail. A somewhat informal combining of *ailorus* with the Greek *phile* (loving) gives the English 'ailurophile'.

> The earliest known depiction of a cat as a domesticated pet comes from a tomb in Egypt dated 2,600 BC. It was the Tomb of Ti – who was a hairdresser to the royal family and therefore very much a VIP – where a small picture was found of a cat wearing a collar, suggesting that by then the cat was allied with the world of humans.

AILUROPHOBE

The opposite of ailurophile – in other words a person who dislikes cats or is even frightened of them. From the Greek *ailuros* (cat) plus *phobe* (fear).

'Cats like doors to be left open –
in case they change their minds.'
ROSEMARY NISBET

THE PUSSYCAT SONG

In Perry Como's big hit at the start of 1949, he was joined by the Fontane Sisters for a novelty song involving a serenading tomcat and his reluctant sweetheart:

'Come yeowt my purrdy pussy,
we could serenade the moon'
'Not neeoww…'

CATMOPOLITAN

In 1987, the magazine *Cosmopolitan* published a one-off mirror image of itself – but entirely concerned with cats. All the advertising consisted of 'cat' versions of standard products, and text articles included witty features on fashions and feline style, beauty tips, food and diet advice, and even letters asking for personal guidance in intimate matters. *Catmopolitan* was a companion to the equally successful *Dogue* – the canine version of another well-known fashion magazine.

CAT MISCELLANY

*'Thou are the Great Cat, the avenger of the
Gods, and the judge of words, and the president
of the sovereign chiefs and the governor
of the holy circle.'*

INSCRIPTION ON THE ROYAL TOMBS AT THEBES

TO A PERSIAN CAT

So dear, so dainty, so demure,
So charming in whate'er position;
By race the purest of the pure,
A little cat of high condition:

Her coat lies not in trim-kept rows
Of carpet-like and vulgar sleekness:
But like a ruffled sea it grows
Of wavy grey (my special weakness):

She vexes not the night with squalls
That make one seize a boot and throw it:
She joins in no unseemly brawls
(At least she never lets me know it!):

She never bursts in at the door
In manner boisterous and loud:
But silently along the floor
She passes, like a little cloud.

Then, opening wide her amber eyes,
Puts an inquiring nose up –
Sudden upon my knee she flies,
Then purrs and tucks her little toes up.

F C W HILEY

'No heaven will not ever heaven be,
Unless my cats are there to welcome me.'

'The playful kitten with its pretty little tigerish
gambols is infinitely more amusing than half the
people one is obliged to live with.'

LADY SYDNEY MORGAN

'Cat litter' is made up from one or several of the following: wood shavings, chaff, dried citrus peel, corncobs, wheat husks, recycled newspapers, finely shredded natural wood or Fuller's Earth (a kind of clay). These basic materials all tend to soak up moisture – but there is often a blend of gentle chemicals added to cut down on possible smells. And a word of warning – some kinds of kitty litter can be a hazard to pregnant women and cause complications, so best to avoid cleaning the litter box during those months.

OLD POSSUM'S BOOK OF PRACTICAL CATS

T S Eliot wrote this book of children's verse in 1939 and it went on sale for 35 cents. Forty-two years later, Andrew Lloyd Webber turned the poems into the musical *Cats*, which opened in May 1981. The musical was translated into 10 languages, and was performed in 300 cities across 26 countries. Within 10 years, *Cats* had done one billion dollars' worth of business. It is somehow hard to imagine that happening with a musical called *Dogs*.

*'Cats are not impure –
they keep watch about us.'*
THE PROPHET MOHAMMED

A CAT IN GLOVES CATCHES NO MICE

Sometimes, to get a job done effectively, you can't be gentle and polite all the time. The saying originates in 14th-century France, and in 1578 appeared in English as 'A cat gloved catches no mice'. It was later popularised by American statesman Benjamin Franklin in *Poor Richard's Almanack* (1733–58).

GRIMALKIN

In the 13th century, a woman of 'low class' was referred to as a *malkin*, sometimes thought to have originated as a diminutive for Matilda. In time, *malkin* became restricted to old women, and then the word moved on to describe cats. Probably echoing the less-than-fashionable appearance of elderly women, the prefix *gri–* (meaning 'grey') was attached. So emerged 'grimalkin' – a grey cat or, eventually, any cat at all. The pet cat of French astrologer and prophet Nostradamus was called Grimalkin, as was the pet of one of *Macbeth*'s witches. Novelist Tracey Fobes was inspired to visualise the grimalkin as a legendary beast of ancient Scotland in her 1998 novel *Touch Not The Cat*.

'The cat with eyes of burning coal,
Now crouches 'fore the mouse's hole.'
GOWER, FROM SHAKESPEARE'S *PERICLES*

'A cat knows your every thought.
Knows, but doesn't care.'

GIB

The beasts of the field – horses, bulls, sheep – have a name for their neutered males (gelding, steer or wether respectively), and so does the cat. Seldom heard nowadays, 'gib' was originally a term for any male cat, used in a long-ago custom of calling male cats 'Gilbert'. This could have arisen c.1400, when the French classic *The Romance of the Rose* was translated into English and the name of the French cat character 'Thibert' acquired the English translation 'Gilbert' – which was then used to describe male cats. Over the following two centuries, a shift of emphasis took place, and 'Gilbert', having been shortened to 'gib', became a reference to a neutered male cat, as referred to in Shakespeare's *Henry IV*: 'I am as melancholy as a gib cat'.

(Later, in 1481, an English translation of the French *Reynard the Fox* also contained a cat character Tybalt, which became the name of a character in *Romeo and Juliet* who is referred to as 'the king of cats'.)

'Purranoia: A condition found in humans who fear that the cat is up to something.'

A neutered female cat is sometimes (but rarely) called a 'spey' or 'spay'.

CAT MISCELLANY

'If a dog jumps into your lap it is because
he is fond of you; but if a cat does the same
thing, it is because your lap is warmer.'
ALFRED NORTH WHITEHEAD

There is a breed of cat in eastern Turkey, near
Lake Van, that likes to swim. The breed's fur
is not as thick as that of other cats so, when
wetted, it dries much more quickly. The cats
frequently take a voluntary dunking in order
to catch frogs in the lake. Brown and white in
colour, their forehead carries a white patch
known as 'The thumbprint of Allah'.

THE PIRATES OF PENZANCE
No cats appear in this Gilbert and Sullivan icon,
but they are not entirely forgotten. The pirates
refer to them in the chorus:

> With cat-like tread,
> Upon our foe we steal
> In silence dread,
> Our cautious way we feel...

... rendered comic in performance when sung by a
dozen men in full voice with orchestral support –
in other words, loudly.

MAX CRYER

'God made the cat in order that man might have the pleasure of caressing the tiger.'
FERNAND MERY

HAS THE CAT GOT YOUR TONGUE?
This curious and supposedly encouraging remark to someone who is remaining silent has a grisly and unpleasant background. Centuries ago, in areas known now as the Middle East, punishment for misdemeanours was more severe and horrific than those now familiar to the Western world. In some contexts, it was common for a ruler to order that a thief be punished by having his hand cut off, and a liar or traitor by having his tongue cut out. Since cats were more highly regarded than thieves or liars, the cut-offs were given to the ruler's pet cats as a treat. In those days, if someone didn't speak and so was asked if the cat had got their tongue, perhaps it had.

THE CAT THAT COMES TO MY WINDOW SILL

The cat that comes to my window sill
When the moon looks cold and the night
is still –

165

He comes in a frenzied state alone
With a tail that stands like a pine tree cone,
And says: 'I have finished my evening lark,
And I think I can hear a hound dog bark.
My whiskers are froze and stuck to my chin.
I wish you'd git up and let me in.'
That cat gits in.

But if in the solitude of the night
He doesn't appear to be feeling right,
And rises and stretches and seeks the floor,
And some remote corner he would explore,
And doesn't feel satisfied because
There's no good spot for to sharpen his claws,
And meows and canters uneasy about
Beyond the least shadow of any doubt
That cat gits out.

BEN KING

When rubbing itself against your leg, the cat isn't necessarily giving the equivalent of a hug or nuzzle. It is in fact seeking reassurance. The cat is checking that the slight scent it deposited on you before you left the house (from little glands in its face and the base of its tail) is still there when you get home.

*'The best way to call a cat is to turn the
handle of a can opener.'*

CURIOSITY KILLED THE CAT

In its original form, this favourite admonition to nosy-parkers had no connection with being curious. The term has been known since the 16th century, when it started out as 'care kills the cat'. The meaning of 'care' in those days had more to do with worrying than with being looked after. Cats, it was deemed, were over cautious and over-careful, and such behaviours brought anxiety, poor health and even death. People, as well as cats, could die from too much 'care'.

Shakespeare acknowledges the expression in *Much Ado About Nothing*: 'Though care killed the cat, thou hast mettle enough in thee to kill care.'

And, although the expression is referred to in Gilbert and Sullivan's *HMS Pinafore* in 1878 ('Once a cat was killed by care, Only brave deserve the fair'), at that time a transition was taking place with that word 'care', and it was eventually replaced with 'curiosity'.

BREAKFAST AT TIFFANY'S

Truman Capote's story (1958) introduced the world to the whimsical young woman called Holiday Golightly (occupation: Travelling) and her cat called, simply, Cat. The movie, made in 1961 and starring Audrey Hepburn as Holly, featured a substantial marmalade-coloured cat as

Cat. Utterly memorable though Audrey Hepburn was, no Oscar came her way – but the cat (real name Orangey) won a 'Patsy' award for his animal acting.

'Ragdoll' is a cat breed originating in California during the 1960s. Its notable characteristic is to become totally limp in the arms of whoever holds it.

'Cats find humans useful domestic animals.'
GEORGE MIKES

THE CAT WHO GOT THE CREAM
A self-evident description, of a cat looking fulfilled and self-satisfied, which can be equally applied to people. There's also 'the cat who got the canary' (bordering on smug or even guilty), or its variation, 'a cat with feathers in its craw', meaning either a capture well made, or with evidence of guilt.

'There is no way of talking to cats that enables one to come off as a sane person.'
DAN GREENBURG

MAX CRYER

OLD DAME GOODY TROT, HER CAT GRIMALKIN AND HER SPANIEL SPOT

Dame Trot and her cat
Sat down for a chat.
The Dame sat on this side,
The puss sat on that.

Puss, says the Dame,
Can you catch a rat?
Or a mouse in the dark?
Purr, says the cat.

Dame Trot came home one wintry night
A shivering starving soul,
But Puss had made a blazing fire
And nicely trussed a fowl.

The Dame was pleased, the fowl was dressed
The table set in place,
The wondrous cat began to carve
And Goody said her grace,

The cloth withdrawn old Goody cries,
I wish we'd liquor too!
Up jumped Grimalkin for some wine,
And soon a cork she drew.

The wine got up in Pussy's head
She would not go to bed,
But purred and tumbled, leapt and danced
And stood upon her head.

Now Goody sorely was fatigued,
Nor eyes could open keep,
So Spot and she and Pussy too
Agreed to go to sleep.

Next morning Puss got up betimes
The breakfast cloth she laid,
And 'ere the village clock struck eight
The tea and toast she made.

Goody awoke and rubbed her eyes,
And drank her cup of tea,
Amazed to see her cat behave
With such propriety.

The breakfast ended, Trot went out,
To see old neighbour Hards
And coming home she found her cat
Engaged with Spot at cards.

Another time the Dame came in
When Spot demurely sat,
Half lathered to the ears and eyes.
Half shaven by the cat.

Grimalkin having shaved her friend
Sat down before the glass,
And washed her face and dressed her hair
Like any modern lass.

A hat and feather then she took
And stuck it on aside,
And o'er her gown of crimson silk
A handsome tippet tied.

Just as her dress was all complete,
In came the good old Dame,
She looked, admired, and curtsied low
... And Pussy did the same.

ROBERT BRANSTON

*'Most of us rather like our cats to have a streak
of wickedness. I should not feel quite easy in the
company of any cat that walked about the house
with a saintly expression.'*

BEVERLY NICHOLS

Hollywood film-maker Julia Phillips (and
author of *You'll Never Eat Lunch in This
Town Again*) named her cat Caesar – so she
could call it Julia's Caesar.

Don't look too shocked if Puss presents a litter in
which several kittens have differing colours – even
different breeds. This is because cats are capable of
superfecundation: fertilisation within the female's
reproductive tract by sperm from more than one
contributor. In this way, if mama has been in a
generous mood her available ova may well be
surrounded by contributions from several
partners... and the result will be a litter of kittens
with different fathers, who are in fact only half-
siblings.

*'A home without a cat, and a well-fed, well-
petted and properly revered cat, may be a perfect
home, perhaps; but how can it prove its title?'*

MARK TWAIN

'Blessed are the purr at heart.'

TO LAND ON ONE'S FEET

A person who is unexpectedly lucky, maybe has frequent good fortune or manages to recover from a disadvantage and rise into a more favourable situation has 'landed' or 'fallen on their feet'. It works on the observation that cats in free-fall have remarkable twisting powers and seem almost always able to land on their feet. Back in the 14th century, the expression read as 'he will land on his legs' but, later, the feet took over.

AN ODE TO EIGHT CATS BELONGING TO ISRAEL MENDEZ
(watching from his window at midnight)

Lo, in my shirt, on you these eyes I fix,
Admiring much the quaintness of your tricks!
Your friskings, crawlings, squalls, I much
    approve;
Your spittings, pawings, high-raised rumps,
Swelled-tails and Merry-Andrews jumps,
With the wild ministrelsy of rapturous love.

How sweetly roll your gooseberry eyes,
As loud you tune your amorous cries,
And loving, scratch each other black and blue!
No boys in wantonness now bang your backs,
No curs, nor fiercer mastiffs, tear your flax,
But all the moonlight world seems made
   for you.

Good gods! Ye sweet love-chanting rams!
How nimble are you with your hams
To mount a house, to scale a chimney top,
And peeping from that chimney hole,
Pour in a doleful cry, the impassioned soul,
Inviting Miss Grimalkin to come up:

Who, sweet obliging female, far from coy,
Answers your invitation note with joy,
And scorning 'midst the ashes more to mope;
Lo! borne on Love's all-daring wing
She mounteth with a pickle-herring spring,
Without the assistance of a rope.

Dear mousing tribe, my limbs are waxing cold –
Singers of Israel sweet, adieu, adieu!
I do suppose you need now to be told
How much I wish that I was one of you.

PETER PINDAR (JOHN WOLCOT)

'Some people say Man is the most dangerous
animal on the planet. Obviously these people
have never met an angry cat.'

LILLIAN JOHNSON

LIKE HERDING CATS

Cats don't herd. So this expression indicates that a
proscribed activity is going to be filled with
frustration and probable futility. Everyone
involved will go in different directions and decline
to co-operate with everyone else. American
technology firm Electronic Data Systems created a
very funny TV and cinema advertisement showing
gnarled, hard-living cowboys expressing their
pride in the skill they have spent a lifetime
achieving: herding cats. The clip shows many cats
being 'herded' – but one has a feeling that these
scenes were faked.

MARIGOLD

She moved through the garden in glory, because
She had very long claws at the end of her paws.
Her back was arched, her tail was high,
A green fire glared in her vivid eye;
And all the Toms, though never so bold,
Quailed at the martial Marigold.

RICHARD GARNETT

CAT MISCELLANY

'What greater gift than the love of a cat?'
CHARLES DICKENS

Cats can purr while breathing in and out, but only domestic cats can do this; their bigger relations, including lions and tigers, don't have the skill.

PUSS

A jury of scholars could not agree on the exact derivation of the familiar word 'puss'. The jury is still out. Its origin may date back several thousand years BC, and come from the Egyptians' name for their cat goddess Bast (also translated as Pasht, Bastet or Basht), which through the passage of centuries may have been modified in English as 'puss'. But another theory points to a very old Lithuanian word, sounding similar to 'puss', which seemed to apply to something furry; for instance, a kind of willow with furry knobbles. That word might have drifted into English in the 16th and 17th centuries to describe the furry willow, and also several other furry animals, before eventually settling on cats only.

At some time, somewhere in Ireland, there was a word sounding similar to 'puss' that meant 'to make a pouting mouth' – and so Ireland is also one possible place of origin. Yet another theory designates 'puss' as an imitative word, being somewhat similar to the sound that a cat itself makes. Or it could have been from an old word *buss* meaning 'mouth, lips, face' – which mysteriously moved on to refer to a whole cat. And there was also a word in ancient English – *pusa* – meaning a bag of the soft and flexible type, which could have been applied to a soft and flexible cat.

These are all theories. We are in Miss Marple territory, and she would have said 'Nobody knows'. But one thing is for sure: the cats don't care.

> John Lennon's pet cat was called Elvis.

PUSSYCAT
Besides the obvious, the term is also used to describe a person who is likeable and gentle – sometimes unexpectedly so, like a behemoth in the business arena or on the sports field, who is 'a pussycat at home'.

> '*People who hate cats will come back as mice in their next life.*'
> FAITH RESNICK

> Cats suffer from cancer, dental decay, influenza, rheumatism, worms, sunburn and even AIDS. But never insomnia.

GROOMING

A cat grooming itself is 'autogrooming'. If it is grooming a friend, it is 'allogrooming'.

Centuries ago, the cats known as Birmans were sacred creatures in the Lao-Tsun temple of the Kmer people in Asia. In the early 1900s, the temple was attacked by marauders, but the priests were helped to overcome the raid by two Western men – Auguste Pavie and Major Gordon Russell. To show their gratitude to the two men, in 1919 the priests sent them a pair of precious Birman cats to France. The male cat did not live, but the female was pregnant and, from her, Birman cats became established in the West.

*'A cat doesn't know what it wants
and wants more of it.'*
RICHARD HEXEM

Human adults in good health can hear noise of 20,000 cycles per second (20kHz). Dogs' ears can identify cycles of up to 40,000 per second (40kHz). Cats leave them all behind – their ears sort out sounds of up to 100,000 per second (100kHz) – including the almost inaudible sounds made by mice. This high-tuned facility often starts to fade after the cat is five years old.

> Victor Hugo, author of *Les Misérables* (1862), called his cat Mouche – French for a 'fly'.

THE RAT-CATCHER AND CATS

The rats by night such mischief did,
Betty was every morning chid:
They undermined whole sides of bacon,
Her cheese was sapped, her tarts were taken;
Her pasties, fenced with thickest paste,
Were all demolished and laid waste:
She cursed the Cat, for want of duty.
Who left her foes a constant booty.

An engineer, of noted skill,
Engaged to stop the growing ill.
From room to room he now surveys
Their haunts, their works, their secret ways;
Finds where they 'scape an ambuscade*,

*Ambuscade is an archaic version of 'ambush'

179

And whence the nightly sally's made.
An envious Cat from place to place,
Unseen, attends his silent pace:

She saw that, if his trade went on,
The purring race must be undone;
So secretly removes his baits,
And every stratagem defeats.
Again he sets the poisoned toils;
And Puss again the labour foils.

'What foe (to frustrate my designs)
My schemes thus nightly countermines?'
Incensed, he cries, 'This very hour
The wretch shall bleed beneath my power.'
So said a ponderous trap he brought,
And in the fact poor Puss was caught.
'Smuggler', says he, 'thou shalt be made
A victim to our loss of trade.'

The captive Cat, with piteous mews,
For pardon, life, and freedom sues.
'A sister of the science spare;
One interest is our common care.'
'What insolence!' the man replied;
'Shall cats with us the game divide?
Were all your interloping band
Extinguished, or expelled the land,
We rat-catchers might raise our fees,
Sole guardians of a nation's cheese!'

A Cat, who saw the lifted knife,
Thus spoke, and saved her sister's life.
'In every age and clime we see,
Two of a trade can ne'er agree.
Each hates his neighbour for encroaching:
Squire stigmatises squire for poaching;
Beauties with beauties are in arms,
And scandal pelts each others' charms;
Kings, too, their neighbour kings dethrone,
In hope to make the world their own.

But let us limit our desires,
Not war like beauties, kings, and squires;
For though we both one prey pursue,
There's game enough for us and you.

JOHN GAY

The precise colouring of a Siamese cat depends less on its parents than on the climate in which it lives.

'Cats are connoisseurs of comfort.'
JAMES HERRIOT

British navigator Matthew Flinders mapped the coast of Australia in 1802 aboard the ship Tryall, accompanied by his remarkable black-and-white cat Trim. During the voyage, Trim learned to swim

and catch a rope. Together, they circumnavigated Australia three times and the world once. Flinders wrote about Trim and his voyaging in 1810, but the story was not published until 1973. A bronze statue of Trim in one of Sydney's main streets was unveiled in 1996.

*'Dogs see God in their owner.
Cats see God in a mirror.'*

Cats possess a set of qualities that give it a homing ability. Lost and far from home, a cat will use a combination of its biological clock, the angle of the sun and the earth's magnetic field to make a path back to its owner's home. These qualities, excellent at finding a familiar place, don't always work so reliably if the owners have moved far away, and it is *people* the cat seeks rather than a *house*.

'*To escort a cat on a leash is against the nature of the cat.*'
ADLAI STEVENSON

CUSTARD

During the 1980s, Custard Cat made her television cartoon debut in Britain. Custard lived next door to a dog, Roobarb, a quiet and unspectacular pooch who nevertheless tried to Do Things. In essence, the series was not unlike Jerry Seinfeld's famous description of his show being 'about nothing'. Nevertheless, *Roobarb and Custard* enjoyed faithful cult status, as Roobarb plodded through his ineffectual plans, and Custard sat on a wobbly fence and laughed at him. When the series finished, a DVD was issued with all thirty of their adventures, and in 2004 it was announced that an entirely new series was being created. Most cartoon characters require what Dr Johnson called 'a suspension of disbelief', as these ones certainly did, since some days Roobarb the dog would decide to be green, while Custard was always bright pink. Viewers loved them.

CAT'S CRADLE
Children play this game by looping string over their fingers and making patterns with twists and turns of their hands. With luck, an established pattern can be passed over on to another child's hands – and the display continues. While the string shapes can (with some imagination) represent a 'cradle', the association with 'cat' is not so straightforward.

The game is ancient and its concept is spread far – widely differing cultures around the world play such games with string. The sun is the connection with 'cat' in the game's name. The sun was depicted as a cat figure in Ancient Egyptian times, constantly fighting the Darkness, and the symbolic association between 'cat' and 'sun' was gradually passed from Egypt to other areas of the Northern Hemisphere. In some areas, the game of twisting and shaping the string was an attempt at influencing the sun; for instance, some northern snow-bound cultures believed that the string 'cradle' might take the sun captive, and thus bring sunshine to them for a longer time.

Another explanation also exists – that, in parts of Europe, a newly married couple would celebrate the first month of their marriage by placing a real cat into a real cradle, which the two of them would then gently rock. This ritual was meant to assist the conception of a child.

Catseyes, the reflective buttons set in roads to guide drivers, were invented by British road-mender Percy Shaw in 1934 and were first used in Brightlington in Yorkshire. Originally, the buttons were described as 'Reflecting Roadstuds', but Shaw soon registered the name Catseye (one word) as a proprietary brand name, owned by his company.

'Cats come and go without ever leaving.'
MARTHA CURTIS

Cats-eye is also the name given to the semi-precious gemstone *Chrysoberyl*, which when cut in a smooth, rounded shape reflects a thin, brightish streak of light resembling the contracted pupil of a cat's eye.

HENRY'S CAT

British viewers first met Henry's Cat in 1983, and his popularity extended over five series. Henry was a likeable cat, prone to day-dreaming – somewhat akin to Walter Mitty, but never so much as to get in the way of the pleasure of eating. In his way, Henry's Cat was smart – he had special earphones that could translate anything into anything else – but his vagueness could cause him trouble, such as when he tried to buy an ice-cream and accidentally finished up in the Foreign Legion. Henry's Cat's best friends were Pansy Pig (whom he rescued from being tied to a railway line by Rum Baba) and Chris Rabbit (with whom he was abducted and taken to the planet Vrerp. (The two of them taught the aliens how to make cakes.)

'If to her share some feline errors fall,
Look in her face and you'll forgive them all.'

The town of Kittyhawk in North Carolina became famous as the venue for the Wright Brothers' sustained power flight in 1903. Less famous is the reason for the town's name, which is derived from a native American (Algonkian) word *chickahauk*, the meaning of which, over the years, has been completely forgotten.

MAX CRYER

'A cat sleeps fat, but walks thin.'
FRED SCHWAB

A CAT IN DISTRESS

A cat in distress,
Nothing more, nor less;
Good folks, I must faithfully tell ye,
As I am a sinner,
It waits for some dinner
To stuff out its own little belly.
You would not easily guess
All the modes of distress
Which torture the tenants of earth;
And the various evils,
Which like so many devils,
Attend the poor souls from their birth.

Some a living require,
And others desire
An old fellow out of the way;
And which is the best
I leave to be guessed,
For I cannot pretend to say.

One wants society,
Another variety,
Others a tranquil life;

187

Some want food,
Others, as good,
Only want a wife.

But this poor little cat
Only wanted a rat,
To stuff out its own little maw;
And it were as good,
SOME people had such food,
To make them HOLD THEIR JAW!

PERCY BYSSE SHELLEY (BELIEVED TO HAVE BEEN
WRITTEN WHEN HE WAS 10 YEARS OLD, IN 1802)

*'The way to keep a cat is to try
and chase it away.'*
E W HOWE

MAX CRYER

CALVIN AND HOBBES

This cartoon strip first appeared in 1985 and its popularity skyrocketed. Its circulation had reached syndication in 2,400 individual newspapers by the time artist Bill Watterson 'retired' the two characters in 1996 and ceased drawing them. By then, 23 million *Calvin and Hobbes* books had been published. Six-year-old Calvin's companion Hobbes is in fact a tiger, but cartoonist Watterson confessed that the character was inspired entirely by his grey tabby cat, Sprite.

> A cat walks by stepping with both its left legs together then both right legs together. Only two other quadrupeds move this way: the camel and the giraffe.

*'A cat keeps discipline and order
by claw enforcement.'*

FROM *THE MANCIPLE'S TALE* (14TH CENTURY)

Let take a cat, and fostre him well with milk
And tendre flesh, and make his couch of silk
And let him see a mouse go by the wall
Anon he waiveth milk and flesh and all

189

And every dainty that is in the house,
Such appetite he has to eat the mouse.
GEOFFREY CHAUCER

Forty per cent of cats are ambidextrous.

*'In my experience, cats and beds seem
to be a natural combination.'*
LOUIS J CAMUTI

President Theodore Roosevelt's pet cat,
Slippers, was allowed to attend official dinners
with him.

FROM THE MANUSCRIPT OF A 9TH-CENTURY IRISH MONK

Myself and Pangur, cat and sage
Go each about our business;
I harass my beloved page,
He his mouse.
Neither bored, both hone
At home a separate skill
Moving after hours alone
To the kill.

On my cell wall here,
His sight fixes, burning,
Searching, my old eyes peer

At new learning,
And his delight when his claws
Close on his prey
Equals mine when sudden clues
Light my way.
So we find by degrees
Peace in solitude,
Both of us solitaries,
Have each the trade he loves:
Pangur, never idle day or night
Hunts mice
I hunt each riddle from dark to light.

'One cat just leads to another.'
ERNEST HEMINGWAY

Cats' paws normally have five toes on the front feet and four on the back.

THE SPINSTER'S SWEET-ARTS
(Her cats are named after spurned long-ago suitors, and are spoken to accordingly...)

Sweet-arts! Molly belike may 'a lighted to-
night upo' one.
Sweet-arts! thanks to the Lord that I niver not
listen'd to noan!

So I sits i' my oan armchair wi' my oan kettle
  theere o' the hob,
An' Tommy the fust, an' Tommy the second,
  an' Steevie an' Rob.
Rob, coom cop 'ere o' my knee. Thou sees
  that i' spite o' the men
I 'a kep' thruf thick an' thin my two 'oonderd
  a-year to mysen;
Yis! thaw tha call'd me es pretty es ony lass i'
  the Shere;
An' thou be es pretty a Tabby, but Robby I
  seed thruf ya theere.

Theere now, what art 'a mewin at, Steevie?
  for owt I can tell –
Robby wur fust to be sewer, or I mowt 'a
  liked tha as well.

Naay – let ma stroak tha down till I maakes
  tha es smooth es silk,
But if I 'ed married tha, Robby, thou'd not 'a
  been worth thy milk,
Thou'd niver 'a cotch'd ony mice but 'a left
  me the work to do,
And 'a taaen to the bottle beside, so es all that
  I 'ears be true;
But I loovs tha to maake thysen 'appy, an' soa
  purr awaay, my dear,
Thou 'ed wellnigh purr'd ma awaay fro' my
  oan two 'oonderd a-year.

Robby, git down wi'tha, wilt tha? let Steevie
coom oop o' my knee.

Steevie, my lad, thou 'ed very nigh been the
Steevie fur me!

Robby wur fust to be sewer,* 'e wur burn an'
bred i' the 'ouse,

But thou be es 'ansom a tabby es iver patted
a mouse.

An' thou was es fond o' thy bairns es I be
mysen o' my cats,

But I niver not wish'd fur childer, I hevn't naw
likin' fur brats;

Alt' a-callin' ma 'hugly' mayhap to my faace,
or a tearin' my gown –

Dear! dear! dear! I mun part them Tommies –
Steevie git down.

Ye be wuss nor the men-tommies, you. I tell'd
ya, na moor o' that!

Tom, lig theere o' the cushion, an' tother Tom
'ere o' the mat.

Theere! Set it down! Now Robby! You
Tommies shall waait to-night

Till Robby an' Steevie 'es 'ed their lap – an' it
sarves ye right.

(ABRIDGED) ALFRED, LORD TENNYSON

*(*sewer* meaning 'sure')

Albert Schweizer, who was left-handed, occasionally chose to write with his right hand because his cat Sizi – for some perverse reason – liked to go to sleep sprawled across his left arm, and the good doctor declined to disturb her.

'Cats cannot be made to do anything useful. Cats are mean for the fun of it.'
P J O'Rourke

'Many centuries ago, cats were believed to be a kind of god. All cats remember this – and consider it still to be true.'

THE RETIRED CAT

A poet's cat, sedate and grave
As poet well could wish to have,
Was much addicted to inquire
For nooks to which she might retire,
And where, secure as mouse in chink,
She might repose, or sit and think.

Sometimes ascending, debonair,
An apple-tree or lofty pear,
Lodged with convenience in the fork,
She watched the gardener at his work;
Sometimes her ease and solace sought
In an old empty wat'ring-pot.

But love of change, it seems, has place
Not only in our wiser race;
Cats also feel, as well as we,
That passion's force, and so did she.
Her climbing, she began to find,
Exposed her too much to the wind,
And the old utensil of tin
Was cold and comfortless within.

She therefore wished instead of those
Some place of more serene repose,
Where neither cold might come, nor air
Too rudely wanton with her hair,
And sought it in the likeliest mode
Within her master's snug abode.

A drawer, it chanced, at bottom lined
With linen of the softest kind,
With such as merchants introduce
From India, for the ladies' use –
A drawer impending o'er the rest,
Half-open in the topmost chest,
Of depth enough, and none to spare,
Invited her to slumber there.

Puss with delight beyond expression
Surveyed the scene, and took possession.
Recumbent at her ease ere long,
And lulled by her own humdrum song,

She left the cares of life behind,
And slept as she would sleep her last,
When in came, housewifely inclined
The chambermaid, and shut it fast.

By no malignity impelled,
But all unconscious whom it held.
Awakened by the shock, cried 'Puss,
Was ever cat attended thus!
The open drawer was left, I see,
Merely to prove a nest for me.
For soon as I was well composed,
Then came the maid, and it was closed.

'How smooth these kerchiefs, and how sweet!
Oh, what a delicate retreat!
I will resign myself to rest
Till Sol, declining in the west,
Shall call to supper, when, no doubt,
Susan will come and let me out.'

The evening came, the sun descended,
And puss remained still unattended.
The night rolled tardily away
With her indeed 'twas never day,
The sprightly morn her course renewed,
The evening gray again ensued,
And puss came into mind no more
Than if entombed the day before.

With hunger pinched, and pinched for room,
She now presaged approaching doom,
Nor slept a single wink, or purred,
Conscious of jeopardy incurred.
That night, by chance, the poet watching
Heard an inexplicable scratching;
His noble heart went pit-a-pat
And to himself he said, 'What's that?'

He drew the curtain at his side,
And forth he peeped, but nothing spied;
Yet, by his ear directed, guessed
Something imprisoned in the chest,
And, doubtful what, with prudent care
Resolved it should continue there.

At length a voice which well he knew,
A long and melancholy mew,
Saluting his poetic ears,
Consoled him, and dispelled his fears:
He left his bed, he trod the floor,
He 'gan in haste the drawers explore,
The lowest first, and without stop
The rest in order to the top.

For 'tis a truth well known to most,
That whatsoever thing is lost,
We seek it, ere it come to light,
In ev'ry cranny but the right.
Forth skipped the cat, not now replete

As erst with airy self-conceit,
And wishing for a place of rest
Anything rather than a chest.

(ABRIDGED) WILLIAM COWPER

*'The problem with cats is that they get
the exact same look on their face whether
they see a moth or an axe murderer.'*
PAULA POUNDSTONE

Ernest Hemingway owned (at various times)
thirty cats. Florence Nightingale owned
double that number.

The Japanese have invented a device called a
'Meowlingual', which claims to be able to
interpret what your cat is 'saying'. It consists of
a little wireless microphone worn on puss's
collar, which transmits signals to a small, palm-
held screen that shows 'sad', 'happy', 'hungry',
'puzzled' – or whatever else the cat might be
'talking' about. You might be told that the cat
has a fur-ball, would like a sofa leg to scratch on,
fancies some cream or has put a dead mouse in
the laundry. Because cats customarily don't 'talk'
as much as dogs do (their device is called a
Bowlingual), the Meowlingual screen can access
other useful applications such as cat astrology,

which gives you daily advice about the cat's destiny, related to its star sign.

'The cat is mightily dignified until the dog comes by.'

It is not uncommon for domestic cats to hold their tail upright when walking. No other species of cat does this; their tails are parallel to the ground, and thus horizontal, or hanging down and slightly tucked in.

'If you gave wings to a cat, it would not condescend to be a bird. It would only be an angel.'
DICK SHAWN

A cat's tongue has little spikes that point backwards, to aid in the fastidious practice of fur-grooming.

I LOVE LITTLE PUSSY, HER COAT IS SO WARM

I love little pussy, her coat is so warm,
And if I don't hurt her she'll do me no harm.
So I'll not pull her tail, nor drive her away,

But pussy and I very gently will play.
I'll stroke her and pat her and give her some
   food,
And pussy will love me, because I am good.

ANON

*'If you put food down and the cat eats, it's
hungry. If it doesn't, it isn't.'*
LARRY MADRID

At various times, prepared cat-foods (based on beef, chicken and fish) have been given rather imaginative names, including: Upstream Dream (salmon); Deep Sea Delight (mackerel); Cluck-a-Doddle-Doo; Fillet Meow; Hook-Line-and-Sinker; Sardines on Rice; Meow Sushi; and Kitty Pizza.

Shakespeare's works include 42 mentions of the cat. The Bible doesn't mention them at all.

*'When my cats aren't happy, I'm not happy.
Not because I care about their mood but
because I know they're just sitting there,
thinking up ways to get even.'*
PENNY WARD MOSER

CAT MISCELLANY

*'There is no snooze button on a
cat who wants breakfast.'*

The accepted wisdom is that cats as we know them were introduced to domestic society approximately 5,000 years ago. But the German artist Albrecht Durer swept such historic restriction aside when, in 1504, he depicted 'The Garden of Eden' with a cat curled up cosily at Eve's feet.

BELL THE CAT

The expression 'to bell the cat' can be found in *Aesop's Fables*, c.550 BC. Some mice are having difficulty seeking food, because of the danger from

a nearby watchful cat. The mice hold a gathering in order to plan a defence strategy. One mouse puts forward the suggestion that a little bell could be placed around the cat's neck or tail, to warn the mice when the cat was approaching. But one wise old mouse came forward to ask which of them would be the brave one: 'Who will bell the cat?' The phrase surfaces in English as early as William Langland's poem *Piers Plowman*, c.1385.

The idea of 'belling a cat' was not really novel. In order to protect songbirds in gardens, cats have been belled for many years. But for a mouse to actually hang the aforementioned bell was James Bond territory, and this is what the expression has come to mean: to undertake a dangerous and risky project in order to disadvantage evil and benefit mankind.

'A cat is a mobile pillow who eats.'

A small bell fitted at a cat's neck has been a traditional way of warning songbirds that doom might be nigh. But some animal experts advise that a smart puss can learn to control a single bell – so anyone wanting to protect their garden birds should put *two* bells on the collar.

CAT MISCELLANY

*'For me, one of the pleasures of cats' company is
their devotion to bodily comfort.'*
SIR COMPTON MACKENZIE

Humans have 30,000 fibres in their aural
nerves. Cats have 40,000. Because a cat is
able to hear tones much higher in pitch
than a human can, there is a school of
thought that a cat will pay attention to you
if you speak to it in the highest falsetto you
can manage.

*'To a cat, "NO" means "Not while
I'm looking".'*

TWO LITTLE KITTENS

Two little kittens, one stormy night,
Began to quarrel, and then to fight;
One had a mouse, the other had none,
And that's the way the quarrel begun.

'I'll have that mouse,' said the biggest cat;
'You'll have that mouse? We'll see about
   that!'
'I *will* have that mouse,' said the eldest son;
'You *shan't* have the mouse,' said the little one.

I told you before 'twas a stormy night
When these two little kittens began to fight;
The old woman seized her sweeping broom,
And swept the two kittens right out of
the room.

The ground was all covered with frost
and snow,
And the two little kittens had nowhere to go;
So they laid them down on the mat at
the door,
While the old woman finished sweeping
the floor.

Then they crept in, as quiet as mice,
All wet with snow, and cold as ice,
For they found it was better, that stormy
night,
To lie down and sleep than to quarrel
and fight.

ANON

For centuries there has been a rumour that
Julius Caesar didn't like cats. We all know
what happened to him.

'It's the cat's house. We just pay the mortgage.'
ANON

CAT'S WHISKER

In the early 1900s radio was not commonplace. But hobbyists and enthusiasts developed a system of tuning in to distant 'wireless waves' using a small structure built around a natural crystal. Over this was stroked a thin, moveable wire, known as a 'cat's whisker'.

The cat's whisker was able to locate radio signals, which had been picked up by an outdoor antenna and conveyed into the crystal. Once located, the rather frail sound was transferred into earphones. With a long antenna and a lot of luck, the cat's whisker could locate signals coming from as far as 200 kilometres away.

Hywel Dda was Prince of Wales in the year 936. Realising that cats were good at pest control and therefore for agriculture in general, the Prince set a range of prices for kittens and cats and instituted punishments for their being stolen or killed. Prices varied according to a cat's age and whether it had established mouse-killing skills. Refunds were possible if a purchased cat proved lackadaisical in the mouse-killing department, or if a female showed no inclination to breed.

'*The cat that sits on a hot stove-lid will never sit down on a hot stove-lid again – but also, she will never sit down on a cold one any more either.*'

MARK TWAIN

A rule imposed on English nuns in 1205 stated 'Ye shall not possess any beast sisters, except only a cat.'

LAST WORDS TO A DUMB FRIEND

Pet was never mourned as you,
Purrer of the spotless hue,
Plumy tail and wistful gaze,
While you humoured our queer ways,
Or outshrilled your morning call
Up the stairs and through the hall –
Foot suspended in its fall –
While, expectant, you would stand
Arched, to meet the stroking hand;
Till your way you chose to wend
Yonder, to your tragic end.

Never another pet for me!
Let your place all vacant be;
Better blankness day by day
Than companion torn away.
Better bid his memory fade,
Better blot each mark he made,

Selfishly escape distress
By contrived forgetfulness,
Than preserve his prints to make
Every morn and eve an ache.

From the chair whereon he sat
Sweep his fur, not wince thereat;
Rake his little pathways out
Mid the bushes roundabout;
Smooth away his talons' mark
From the claw-worn pine-tree bark,
Where he climbed as dusk embrowned
Waiting us who loitered round.

Still retain I, troubled, shaken,
Mean estate, by him forsaken;
Housemate, I can think you still
Bounding to the window-sill,
Over which I vaguely see
Your small mound beneath the tree,
Showing in the autumn shade
That you moulder where you played.

(ABRIDGED) THOMAS HARDY

Elizabeth Taylor's favourite cat had the name
Jeepers Creepers.

'A country man between two lawyers is like a fish
between two cats.'
(ATTRIBUTED TO) BENJAMIN FRANKLIN

Sphynx cats quite naturally have no hair. The breed was developed in Canada in 1966 and, although hairless, they are so warm to the touch that they are sometimes called 'hot-water-bottle cats'.

You can't catch fish without getting
your paws wet.

CATS AT SEA
In spite of their well-known caution about close contact with water, there has long been an association between cats and boats. Many nautical terms, often originating with sailing ships, involve the cat and are commonly used by seafaring folk.

CAT-O'-NINE-TAILS
A whip. In days gone by, seamen were flogged by a nasty device made up of three separate knottings of three stands attached to the whip's handle. The strands may or may not have been made from the hide of cats, but the weals left on the flesh of he who was punished certainly resembled an attack from a large and vicious cat.

209

CAT'S-PAW

A common description for ripples on water, caused by a light breeze gently sweeping across surface water and causing transitory ruffling.

CAT-HEADS

Short horizontal beams projecting from each side of a ship's bow, over which the anchor is hoisted clear of the water and secured. The association of the structure's name with 'cat' may or may not derive from a Danish word for a big pulley (*katblok*) or maybe from the Latin for 'chain' (*catena*). Either way, the cat-head beam often had the face of a cat carved on it.

Because of their position, the cat-heads were also the source of another nautical tradition: they were customarily used as a lavatory. Suspended as it is directly over water, the cat-head provides support for direct discharge, and has a convenient natural wave-flushing system. (The ideal motive force for sailing ships was a wind from behind – hence products dispersed at the front of the ship were blown away from the rest of the ship, whereas any 'discharge' from the stern would be swept forwards over everyone.)

So arose the (abbreviated) expression 'going to the heads'. Long after these sailing ships were a thing of the past, seamen referring to a toilet retained the description 'the heads' and the expression is sometimes heard beyond the sea. But the original is plural – referring to the 'head' apparently identifies the speaker as a landlubber.

CAT TACKLE
The strong rope or cable which draws the anchor from the water and towards the cat-head to secure it (sometimes called the 'handy billy').

CAT THE ANCHOR
When a ship's anchor has been drawn up from the water ('weighed'), it needs to be kept clear of the ship. To 'cat' the anchor is to hitch it into a horizontal position and secure it against the hull of the ship.

CATBOAT
Some sea-going terms vary in meaning from place to place. 'Catboat' is a strange one because it has two distinct meanings – more or less the opposite of each other. In one, the 'catboat' is a strong vessel for carrying up to 600 tons of coal or timber. But in contemporary times the term 'catboat' is more often applied to a small single-masted leisure craft.

The context in which the word appears usually makes clear which of the two meanings is intended.

WHISKERS
Used in shipping terms, these are long spars that project from either side of the bow. They hold the 'whisker stays', which are ropes or cables supporting the bowsprit (the spar running from the front of the bow).

'Prowling his own quiet backyard or asleep by the fire, he is still only a whisker away from the wild.'
JEAN BURDEN